The Trafficking of Persons

PETER LANG
New York • Washington, D.C./Baltimore • Bern
Frankfurt am Main • Berlin • Brussels • Vienna • Oxford

Kimberly A. McCabe

The Trafficking of Persons

National and International Responses

PETER LANG
New York • Washington, D.C./Baltimore • Bern
Frankfurt am Main • Berlin • Brussels • Vienna • Oxford

Library of Congress Cataloging-in-Publication Data

McCabe, Kimberly A.
The trafficking of persons: national and international responses /
Kimberly A. McCabe.
p. cm.
Includes bibliographical references and index.
1. Human trafficking. 2. Human trafficking—Prevention.
3. Prostitution. 4. Child prostitution. I. Title.
HQ281.M34   364.15—dc22   2007043476
ISBN 978-0-8204-6327-8

Bibliographic information published by **Die Deutsche Bibliothek**.
Die Deutsche Bibliothek lists this publication in the "Deutsche
Nationalbibliografie"; detailed bibliographic data is available
on the Internet at http://dnb.ddb.de/.

Cover design by Clear Point Designs

The paper in this book meets the guidelines for permanence and durability
of the Committee on Production Guidelines for Book Longevity
of the Council of Library Resources.

Printed in the United States of America

For Jamie

CONTENTS

· 1 ·

HUMAN TRAFFICKING DEFINED

You Mi Kim, a twenty-two-year-old small-town girl from South Korea, worked in a sex trafficking triangle that began in South Korea, moved to Los Angeles, California, and then moved to San Francisco. Kim was forced to have sex with dozens of men on a weekly basis in massage parlors and hotels. She lived under the surveillance of guards and cameras and was reminded often of the dangers she and her family would face if she attempted to leave. Kim never sought help from law enforcement (May, 2006).

Jose Tecum, a Florida man, kidnapped a young girl from his native Guatemalan village, brought her to Florida, destroyed her identification card, forced her to pick tomatoes, and raped her repeatedly. The young girl, although seen by many, never reported this abuse. She was discovered after Tecum was arrested for domestic violence. Tecum was sentenced to nine years in prison by a U.S. federal court for kidnapping and slavery (Lush, 2004).

Paul is a young man from Mexico who followed his American girlfriend to South Carolina. Paul works more than sixty hours per week in a meat-packing plant. His girlfriend, who took his fraudulent travel papers when he arrived, picks up his paycheck every Friday and threatens to call immigration officials if Paul does not provide the money to pay their bills. On many occasions, law enforcement has been called to the home he shares with his girlfriend and their son in response to domestic disturbances. Several times, there have been signs of visible injury on Paul; however, he maintains that his girlfriend has never assaulted him. Paul's fear of being deported and having to leave his son behind in America with an abuser has left him a victim of abuse and coercion and a virtual prisoner in his home.

Each of these cases demonstrates the existence of slavery and shows the outcomes of human trafficking. In each case, there exist a victim and an offender who profits from the abuse and torture of the victim. In each case the victim perceives himself or herself as defenseless, perceives a lack of support from U.S. authorities and, thus, never attempts to report the abuse to law enforcement. In each case, the perpetrator would most likely continue the abuse until the victim is no longer useful. In each case, the perpetrator received some benefit from human trafficking.

Minimum-wage workers, entertainment girls, and seasonal migrant workers are all parts of the United States' capital economy. Goods and services are required, money is exchanged, and profits are made on a daily basis. Unfortunately, behind some American prosperity is the victimization of those individuals unable to speak for themselves. On a daily basis, individuals are sexually abused, prohibited from obtaining medical services, and beaten because the quantity or quality of their work for the day was not at the level expected by their employer. Every day individuals are trafficked. Which country would allow such abuse? Which country would allow such persecution of its inhabitants? The answer is the United States of America.

Purpose of This Book

This book, *Human Trafficking: National and International Responses*, is dedicated not only to the subject of human trafficking, the types of human trafficking, and discussions of the conditions and explanations of human trafficking but also to discussions on U.S. and international responses to combat and end all forms of human trafficking.

In this text, human trafficking is explored in terms of its purpose and its victims. In particular, through this text, readers will be able to (1) discuss the various types of human trafficking, including its victims and perpetrators; (2) discuss general statistics relating to human trafficking and provide explanations as to why these statistics are only estimates of the problem and not actual numbers of cases; (3) discuss U.S. legislation relating to human trafficking and reasons officials of the United States felt, and still feel, that human trafficking is a topic worthy of time and resources; (4) discuss the tier system of categorizing countries in terms of their efforts to end trafficking; and (5) discuss international responses to human trafficking.

This book is organized to provide information on the following topics: Chapter 1—Human Trafficking Defined; Chapter 2—Sex Trafficking; Chapter 3—Labor Trafficking; Chapter 4—Entering the United States and U.S. Responses; Chapter 5—Child Trafficking; and, Chapter 6—National and International Efforts. The appendices provide empirical information on country comparisons relating to the Department of State's tier system of country classifications and information on Mexico, the country most closely related to the United States and the country with the largest immigrant population within the boundaries of the United States. Within each chapter are sidebars containing notes and thoughts. At the end of each chapter, there are questions formulated from the materials presented in the chapters as well as questions designed to stimulate discussions beyond text materials on the subject of human trafficking. The aim of this book is to provide not only a knowledge base on the subject of human trafficking but also support to those agencies and organizations across the globe that are attempting to end human trafficking.

Background

According to the U.S. Department of State's 2005 Trafficking in Persons report, more than 700,000 people are trafficked across international borders every year and more and more of those individuals are now being trafficked into the United States for either forced labor or sexual exploitation. Rates of human trafficking, often included in the "dark figure" of unreported crimes, are estimated on the basis of known cases of trafficking in persons and of information obtained through comparisons of legal and illegal immigrants. Therefore, with limited information available on the victims of human trafficking, the United States is only beginning to recognize victims of human trafficking, and the details in terms of their demographic characteristics are essentially unknown.

The Department of State's estimates suggest that approximately 70% of the victims of human trafficking are female and approximately 50% of the victims are under the age of eighteen. In terms of historical legislation, human trafficking is clearly a human rights violation; however, its effect goes beyond individual outcomes and criminal activity as human trafficking promotes the breakdown of family and social systems, fuels organized crime, and deprives countries of their most precious resource—human capital. Human trafficking goes beyond the relationship between victim and offender. Human trafficking is an act with global consequences.

> The U.S. State Department estimates that 14,500 to 17,500 people are trafficked to the United States annually.

As stated, the purpose of this text is to provide a background on the subject of trafficking in the United States and throughout the world; however, before one can begin to study any phenomenon, one must first define it. This chapter provides not only a definition of the phrase "human trafficking" but also a history of human trafficking and an overview of explanations for human trafficking.

Human Trafficking Defined

The United Nations has defined human trafficking as "the recruitment, transfer, harboring or receipt of persons by threat or use of force." Individuals are generally trafficked for one of two reasons: labor or sex. Labor trafficking exists in three forms: (1) bonded, (2) forced, and (3) child. Victims of labor trafficking vary. Some victims enter the country legally; some illegally. Some labor trafficking victims are very young, and others not. Some labor trafficking victims are abused sexually others are not. Victims of labor trafficking can be male or female. Victims of sex trafficking may be forced into prostitution, pornography, military prostitution, spousal prostitution, and/or sex ring tours.

Unfortunately, many nations have misunderstood the definition of human trafficking and failed to recognize the incidents of trafficking that have occurred within their own geographical borders. As a result, in October 2000, Congress passed and President Bill Clinton signed the Trafficking Victims Protection Act (TVPA) in an attempt to provide a comprehensive definition of trafficking and to address the issues relating to human trafficking on the national and international levels (U.S. Department of State, 2004). However, as with most legislative action, this Act was in response to an already identified and existing criminal action. Human trafficking is not new to the United States.

> Trafficking Victims Protection Act (11 STAT. 1466)
>
> The purpose of this Act was to combat trafficking in persons, a contemporary manifestation of slavery whose victims are predominately women and children, to ensure just and effective punishment of traffickers, and to protect their victims.

After the 2000 TVPA, as cases of human trafficking in the United States became more prevalent, more legislation was enacted. Specifically, in 2003 President George W. Bush signed the amended Trafficking Victims Protection Reauthorization Act (TVPRA), which further strengthened the U.S. government's response to human trafficking by recognizing the needs of the victims of human trafficking. In 2005, President Bush again supported the TVPRA and issued proclamations of the United States' support to end this activity. In particular, in the TVPRA, a new phrase, "severe forms of trafficking," was adopted. For clarity, severe forms of trafficking always include the recruitment, harboring, and so on of a person under one of the following three conditions: (1) human trafficking for labor, (2) human trafficking for commercial sex acts, and (3) human trafficking in those under the age of eighteen. In addition, as clarified in the TVPRA, human trafficking does not require that a victim cross an international border or that the victim be identified as an illegal alien. Individuals who want to be transported to the United States or individuals born in the United States may be victims of human trafficking. The passage of the TVPA and the TVPRA signaled the U.S. government's commitment to recognize those individuals trafficked as victims and to work to prevent human trafficking. For clarity, in this text and for discussions throughout, the definition of trafficking of persons does not require the crossing of international borders or movement at all, but it must contain an element of force and a limitation on the victim's movement.

> Trafficking Victims Protection Reauthorization Act (H.R. 2620)
>
> The purpose of this Act is to amend the Trafficking Victims Protection Act in areas of (1) cooperation between foreign governments and nongovernmental organizations, (2) provision of assistance for family members of victims of trafficking in the United States, and (3) certification of victims of severe forms of trafficking in persons.

The trafficking of persons, although different from smuggling, is often identified as "people smuggling." People smuggling is also a growing problem in the United States as it has quickly become one of the preferred trades for criminal networks, especially the Mexican-based networks attempting to bring illegal immigrants into the United States (IOM, 1999). Trafficking is a distinct activity, as the trafficking of persons involves exploitation. Smuggling simply implies enabling the entry into a state of which that person is not a permanent resident (Interpol, 2004). In smuggling, the move is always transnational. Human trafficking may occur even if the victims are moved within the same country. With smuggling, coercion is not an element; those individuals smuggled have freedom of movement and to change employment, which is not the case in human trafficking (U.S. Department of State, 2005). Human trafficking is not smuggling; however, the reality of some smuggling cases provides support for their being considered human trafficking cases. Today, as recognized by the United Nations' Definition of Trafficking Protocol, consent to leave one country and work in another country does not determine the line between smuggling and human trafficking. If the initial consent of the victim to leave one country for another was gained through deception or coercion, then consent is irrelevant and human trafficking has occurred.

In most cases of smuggling, once individuals reach their geographic destination, their relationship with their smuggler is essentially terminated. This is not the case with human trafficking. However, as both involve movement of immigrants into the United States, they are often confused by the public and by U.S. government officials.

In July 2004, the secretary of state, the secretary of homeland security, and the attorney general created the Human Smuggling and Trafficking Center to serve as a fusion center for information on human smuggling and trafficking. As suggested, the freedom to end one's relationship with their trafficker does not end once the destination is reached. Often, in human trafficking cases, once victims reach their destination, their relationship with their trafficker is just beginning and it may continue for years as victims are forced to repay not only their passage expenses into the country but also any other costs that their traffickers feel they owe. In some cases, smuggled individuals are placed in situations from which escape is not an option; thus, their identity changes from smuggled individual to trafficking victim (Munro, 2006). This distinction between smuggling and trafficking is important not only in that there are different dynamics in play but also because persons who have been smuggled are not eligible for services now provided (by legislation) to victims of human trafficking.

It is also important to state that a child under the age of eighteen (regardless of country of origin) cannot give his or her consent to be moved from one country to another; thus, another type of human trafficking—child trafficking—is identified. In addition, the parent or guardian of the child cannot give consent to the trafficker of that child for his or her movement for the purposes of forced labor or sexual exploitation (UNODC, 2006).

Maria purchased fraudulent documents in Mexico City and entered the United States. She began working for a family in South Texas. Was Maria smuggled or trafficked?

(Maria was smuggled into the United States. She chose to leave Mexico and entered the United States illegally.)

Later Maria left the family she first worked for and began housekeeping for a single male neighbor. In addition to making her clean his house, her new "employer" forced Maria to sleep in his bed and provide him sex. He refused to pay her and threatened to call Immigration if she protested. Was Maria smuggled or trafficked?

(At the point when Maria is forced to work and threatened with a call to Immigration, Maria is a victim of trafficking.)

In this text, human trafficking is explored in terms of its multiple purposes and its victims. Discussed are the major reasons for human trafficking, including labor and sex, as well as child victims and national and international responses. The text provides information to build up a knowledge base on the subjects of (1) sex trafficking (including its prevalence and possibility); (2) labor trafficking (including the distinction between bonded and forced labor); (3) the legislative responses to human trafficking by the United States; (4) child trafficking; and (5) national and international programs and practices to end human trafficking and to provide assistance to the victims of human trafficking and punishment to the offenders in human trafficking cases.

History of Human Trafficking in the United States

As trafficking includes the forced movement of people for work, the history of trafficking in the world parallels the history of slavery in the United States, with trafficking/slavery existing, then being questioned, and then being ended (or significantly reduced).

The sale, movement, and confinement (or trafficking) of individuals is documented in biblical times, when women and children were the more likely victims of trade in a patriarchal system of authority. Slavery was introduced to the United States before the country was established as the United States as the colonial British colonies in North America imitated the labor practices of the Spanish colonies in South America (Braudel, 2001). Therefore, African slavery in North America originated not in Africa or in the Southern regions of the United States but in the area between the two continents of Africa and North America—Europe (Berlin, 1998). African slavery was the product of cooperation between Africans and Europeans. The individuals introduced to North America (the New World) were the by-products of these relationships. African slavery, in its different degrees of bondage, was first practiced along the coastal areas of the New World.

The first African slaves arrived in the Spanish-settled area of what today is called South Carolina in the mid-1500s. In the early 1600s, the English colonists of Virginia incorporated slaves into their labor force as the first blacks were sold in Jamestown, Virginia, as indentured servants. Originally, the slaves in the American colonies were mostly white and from Europe, with several being either captured soldiers or convicted criminals.

Like their counterparts in Virginia and South Carolina, the colonists of the North began their societies with slaves; however, their slaves were fewer in number (Berlin, 1998). Africans who were unfit for labor on a plantation were sold at Northern ports. The Northerners, preferring the young blacks from the West Indies to those directly from Africa, essentially bought whatever or whoever was available (Piersen, 1988). Later, still unhappy with their African selection of slaves, merchants in the North established trade routes for slaves from Madagascar, Guinea, the West Indies, and Barbados (Piersen, 1988). Thus, the desire for particular types of slaves, not unique to the cultures of today, led the colonists to target and facilitate the forced movement of specific individuals from their countries to North America.

During the seventeenth century, the enslavement of Native Americans was also common in the American colonies, and in many cases these Native American slaves were trafficked to the West Indies, New York, and New England (Gallay, 2002). This view of slavery as a necessary element for the development of the country began to change in the mid-1700s as the Quakers attempted to persuade others that slavery was evil. However, much of the negative view of slavery focused on the slavery of black individuals. As skin color was, and still is, among the characteristics most commonly used to distinguish individuals, only black individuals were identified as slaves. This acknowledgment of slavery as wrong began the process of restoring justice to black Americans but had little or no effect on the nonblack slaves.

At the same time, across the globe in India, Japan, and other countries, adults and children were sold and moved to work throughout Europe and Asia for either sex or labor. As time passed, public attention turned toward child abuse and the selling of children began to diminish as well as the number of cases involving child trafficking (or at least the number of cases within public view). At the same time, Eastern Europe began promoting free travel and young white females were the main prize of the sex trade. Given the poverty and oppression of Eastern Europe, few negative reactions were expressed regarding the sexual exploitation of the "Russian" women who wanted a way out of their country and, in many cases, into the United States. These Russian women were first moved to the countries of Europe and Asia to begin new lives as sex workers and slaves.

The American War of Independence gave black slaves the ammunition to challenge bondage and form new ties with their slaveholders (Berlin, 1998). Following the Revolutionary War, some of the new states began writing constitutions that prohibited African slavery. In particular, the Massachusetts Constitution abolished slavery in that state and the Arizona Organic Act abolished slavery in the Arizona Territory.

To a large extent, the combined slave and slaveholder warfare of the American Revolution illuminated the similarities and not the differences between blacks and whites. In those cases in which slaves and slaveholders could not work together, the slaves could hide themselves among the marching soldiers or become soldiers to escape slavery. The Declaration of Independence, not distinguishing between blacks and whites, provided a foundation for some lawmakers to begin rethinking society. The issue of slavery presented an inhumane approach to life, and many Americans were concerned that individuals who were not born in the country but were forced to come to America and live and work there would be disruptive to society (Williams, 1994). This rethinking of slavery led to freedom for many blacks by the early 1800s, and as much as 74% of the Northern black population was free, compared with 40% of the population in the late 1700s (Berlin, 1998).

The slavery of Native Americans did not elicit the same concern as that of the African American slaves, since Native Americans were not black

Americans. In particular, not only did Native Americans not have the physical characteristics of black slaves but often they also did not have share the religion of the slave owner; thus, they were viewed at best as different from Americans and at worst as savages. Therefore, the newly explored West's use of Native Americans as slaves continued to be organized in Mexican California and to exist until California was recognized as a state and outlawed the slavery of Native Americans (Beasley, 1918). Hence, similar in conditions to the "Russian" women throughout Europe and Asia, the Native Americans in North America were not considered slaves by lawmakers as they did not look like slaves. Native Americans were not considered slaves by lawmakers until the practice of enslaving Native Americans was brought to the attention of the public. Russian women, who looked like other European women or American women, did not appear to be slaves; thus, in most cases, they were not considered slaves.

Before the Civil War, the ending of slavery in the Northern regions was transforming the North and affecting the slave states of the South. Most black Northerners lived in the cities but did not prosper from industrial employment as many were forbidden to work in the workshops of the factories. In the South, black slaves were forced into hard manual labor on plantations; however, their male masters were expected to provide for their needs and for those of the women and children of the family and any dependents (Berlin, 1998). Thus, this dichotomized view of black America between the North and the South shaped lives in a very region-specific manner on the eve of the Civil War.

In 1865, with the passage of the Thirteenth Amendment, slavery—or at least the state-sanctioned practice of slavery—was abolished in the United States. In 1874, in response to the number of parentless immigrant children in America, Congress adopted the Padrone Statute to address the practice of kidnapping young boys in Italy to be used as musicians and beggars on the streets of America (Beeks & Amir, 2006). In 1910, the Mann Act was imposed to bring stricter penalties to those found guilty of trafficking women into the United States for prostitution, and, in 1948, Congress criminalized the practice of involuntary servitude (Beeks & Amir, 2006). However, there are many who suggest that slavery in the United States has never ended.

In 2000, the U.S. government passed the TVPA, thus committing the government to acknowledge human trafficking and begin focused efforts against it. In 2003, the U.S. passed the TVPRA, committing the government to further support anti-trafficking efforts aimed at protecting and providing assistance to victims and at penalizing offenders. In December 2004, the Federal Bureau of

Investigation launched the National Hispanic Sex Trafficking Initiative to end the sex trafficking of female victims into the United States from Mexico and Central America. Through this initiative are targeted cases involving Hispanic sex trafficking operations, as enforcement efforts attempt to identify and prosecute major offenders and organizations in those sex trafficking rings.

Human trafficking is now a subject of interest for legislators, researchers, and the general public in America. Across the globe and in the United States, human trafficking is a crime drawing national and international attention.

> In 1999, Ramiro and Juan Ramos (brothers) were discovered smuggling and trafficking illegal workers from Mexico into the United States. The Ramos brothers were charged with smuggling workers into the country, monitoring the workers twenty-four hours a day, and charging them inflated rents for substandard housing. In 2002, a federal judge in Florida sentenced the brothers to twelve years in prison (Lush, 2004).

In the early 1990s, it was suggested that thirty million Asian women had been sold worldwide since the mid-1970s (Mirkinson, 1997). The United Nations estimates that four million people are victims of international trafficking each year. In 1999, in response to the increasingly evident problem of trafficking in persons, the United Nations Office on Drugs and Crime (UNODC), in cooperation with the United Nations Interregional Crime and Justice Research Institute (UNICRI), implemented the Global Programme Against Trafficking (GPAT) in Human Beings. GPAT attempts not only to explain the causes and conditions behind the smuggling and trafficking of human beings but also to assist in providing training to law enforcement and other criminal justice practitioners to better recognize cases of human trafficking within their jurisdictions and to foster awareness and prevention efforts. Until recently, the United States has been less visible as a site of trafficking than other countries; however, this is no longer the case, and the idea of slavery as something that is outside the United States is changing.

Today, thousands of individuals are trafficked into the United States, just as was the case with African American slaves. These new "slaves" are from Latin America, Mexico, countries of the former Soviet Union, and Southeast Asia (Raymond & Hughes, 2001). These new slaves are victimized by force through rape, beatings, or confinement, by fraud involving false offers of employment or marriage if they will come to the United States, and/or by coercion that involves threats of violence against the victims or the victims' families or threats of the legal processes (such as deportation) of the United States.

Although it is impossible to determine an exact count of these trafficked individuals, it is suggested that the United States has 10,000 or more forced laborers at any given time (Doyle, 2006). A review of certain occupations suggests that it is impossible to discover the "employment," as these new slaves work in forced prostitution, quarries, sweatshops, farms, or as domestics. With the new phrase "white slavery," we now have a label to describe our European, Asian, and Latin American victims who are trafficked to the United States for sex or labor. Of course, not all U.S. victims of human trafficking are white.

> On April 29, 1825, in Franklin County Georgia, Wyatt Allen sold his wife, a white woman named Hannah Andrews Allen, to Thomas Hervill for $25(Genealogy.com, 1999).

Reasons for Human Trafficking

Human trafficking begins with the abduction or recruitment of a person (UNODC, 2006). It continues with the transportation of the person his or her place of origin to his or her destination and is followed by the exploitation of the individual. The final phase in the human trafficking process is profit laundering (UNODC, 2006). Of course, to increase the profit for the trafficker, the exploitation is repeated multiple times and with multiple victims.

The reason for human trafficking is the same as for trafficking drugs or firearms-money. Through the trafficking of people, traffickers receive great financial gains. According to the United Nations, human trafficking is the third-largest criminal enterprise, with an estimated $9.5 billion generated annually (U.S. Department of State, 2005). How can one not consider the criminal activity of human trafficking?

In major recent trafficking cases in the United States, the traffickers grossed from $1 million to $8 million in a period ranging from one to six years (Richard, 1999). Traffickers typically charge the victims inflated prices for securing their alleged jobs, travel documentation, transportation, food, clothing, and lodging. Largely uneducated, unfamiliar with the language, and heavily indebted to the trafficking rings, victims are forced to sell drugs or prostitute themselves to repay their debts. The better question to consider on the subject of human trafficking is "Why does human trafficking flourish?"

Explanations may be simpler than most researchers acknowledge. The first explanation is related to poverty and the desire for a better life. Often the home life of a trafficking victim is one of poverty and despair. In many cases, women will agree to leave their countries on promises of employment or marriage only to discover that the promises were not true. The same is true with parents who feel that the only option for a better life for their child is to send that child to another country for work and the opportunity for an education. In these cases, the parents are often compensated slightly and the child begins his or her life of slavery. In other cases, parents are desperate for money and will sell their children with no questions asked. The buying and selling of babies under the umbrella of adoption is another extension of trafficking as children may be sold or stolen from their birth family and then sold either for adoption or for exploitation (Richard, 1999). Childless couples are often desperate for children. Those involved in the trafficking of children for adoption realize that this desire often leads to large payments for a baby. The traffickers will provide a baby.

A second explanation for the flourishing of trafficking is ignorance of the consequences of trafficking (U.S. Department of State, 2003a). As trafficking is often misunderstood and mislabeled as smuggling, it is perceived that there are no victims. If the person who chooses to be "smuggled" is victimized, then it is perceived as his or her fault. The notion that trafficking is a crime with victims is often not considered. The victims are perceived as illegal immigrants who should not be in this country; therefore, they should not benefit from the social or criminal justice systems in place in the United States. Another cause of the public's and law enforcement's ignorance on trafficking cases is the limited number of reported cases. Victims of human trafficking, threatened by their traffickers, are unable or unwilling to come forward for fear of deportation. Without the resources to hire and train ethnic female officers for undercover work and to facilitate the victims' communications with the authorities, the law enforcement agency is essentially on wait for reports of human trafficking (Richard, 1999).

The demand for cheap labor is a third explanation for the flourishing of trafficking. Unfortunately, in U.S. businesses, profit is everything, and cheap (or even free) labor only increases the profits (Richard, 1999). Custodial or housekeeping services are common occupations for victims of labor trafficking. Specifically, under the guise of housekeeping, women and men are forced to work long hours, with their pay often going to job placement agencies that, in turn, give the housekeepers or maids only a percentage of their salaries. These victims, kept in line by threats, intimidation, and/or physical violence, continue in the arrangement (U.S. Department of State, 1997). As a manufacturer seeks the most cost-effective way to operate a business, the possibility of using trafficked workers is an attractive option. Human trafficking provides employers with workers who will work long hours and not complain. The trafficked victims (employees) are not taxed; thus, there is no documentation to support their employment, and they do not require the health and insurance benefits demanded by American workers or documented immigrants.

The demand for sex is a fourth explanation for trafficking. As individuals seek men, women, and children for sexual exploitation, the trafficking of persons provides those individuals. One common method of recruiting women for sex trafficking is the use of ads in local newspapers offering jobs in the United States as nannies, waitresses, hostesses, or dancers (Bell, 2001). Once the women have been identified, they are moved to the destination country and their traffickers confiscate their tourist visas. These women must then prostitute themselves to pay off their debts. To illustrate further the similarities between human trafficking and the historic African slave trade, in both cases it is unusual for victims not to be auctioned. Unlike prostitution, where the same individuals are available from day to day, victims of human trafficking, because of the level of threat and control, are rotated in and out of geographical areas; thus, there is less chance of a particular victim being identified and the customers receive variety in their choice of sexual partners.

The low risk of identification of cases of human trafficking, the limited experience of the U.S. criminal justice system in prosecuting cases of human trafficking, and the minimal penalties for traffickers are all reasons for the flourishing of human trafficking (U.S. Department of State, 2003b). Human trafficking cases may not be reported because of geographical biases, political emphases, the nonrecognition of different forms of exploitation, the lack of systems for victim identification or referral, the absence of multilateral operations, and the confusion between a trafficked person and other forms of irregular migration (UNODC, 2006).

Finally, one cannot discount the impact of organized crime in human trafficking. On the basis of cases reported by the UNODC (2006), there exists strong evidence to suggest the involvement of organized criminal units in the Philippines, Afghanistan, Malaysia, and China, among other countries. The structure of these organized crime syndicates has four levels: level 1 includes those persons whose identity in the unit is not well known, although they are often well-known and powerful individuals in their countries; level 2 includes those individuals who receive orders from the first level and pass those orders to the third level; level 3 includes those involved in the actual trafficking of an individual, such as the pimps, madams, and brothel owners; and level 4 includes the "errand boys" who arrange transportation, buy food for the victims, and identify new victims.

Although the United States and other countries are reacting to the phenomenon of human trafficking, there has been little response from criminal justice systems in the past. Today, the criminal networks involved in human trafficking are so secretive that identifying, arresting, and prosecuting such perpetrators is a relatively new action. In a nutshell, the law enforcement officer, the prosecutor, the judge, and the juries often do not understand cases of human trafficking.

Summary

The United Nations has defined human trafficking as "the recruitment, transfer, harboring or receipt of persons by threat or use of force." Individuals are generally trafficked for either labor or sex. After the 2000 TVPA, as cases of human trafficking in the United States became more prevalent, more legislation was enacted. Specifically, in 2003, President George W. Bush signed the amended TVPRA, which strengthened the U.S. government's response to human trafficking by recognizing the needs of victims of human trafficking.

The U.S. Department of State has estimated that between 14,500 and 17,500 people are trafficked into the United States annually. Victims of human trafficking are forced into prostitution, pornography, or forced labor through threats and intimidation. They are often held against their will and denied even bare necessities such as food, clothing, and shelter. Unfortunately, without the English-speaking ability to seek help from the authorities, these victims of human trafficking remain victims for quite a while—some for the rest of their lives.

Human trafficking begins with the abduction or recruitment of a person, continues with the transportation of the person from his or her place of origin to his or her destination, and ends with the exploitation of the individual. Victims of human trafficking come from many different demographics. Many are lured by promises of a better life in the United States. According to reports by the United Nations, human trafficking is the third-largest criminal enterprise, after drug trafficking and the trafficking of guns. The following chapters discuss human trafficking for sex and labor, the trafficking of children, and U.S. and international responses to human trafficking and "best practices" in combating human trafficking.

Questions on Chapter 1

1. How is human trafficking defined?
2. How is the 2000 TVPA different from the 2003 TVPRA?
3. What constitutes "severe trafficking" and why was this new term necessary?
4. How is human trafficking different from human smuggling? Is this distinction important in terms of studying human trafficking? Why?
5. To what does the phrase "white slavery" refer?

Questions for Further Thought

1. Given the incidence and prevalence of other crimes in the United States, is human trafficking really a concern?
2. Why was it necessary to redefine or provide specific criteria of focus in the 2000 TVPA?
3. What are the issues behind the specific identification of severe trafficking?
4. Why should it matter if an individual is trafficked or smuggled into the United States?
5. If you were interested in services from a prostitute, would it matter to you if your prostitute was a victim of human trafficking?

· 2 ·

SEX TRAFFICKING

In discussions of human trafficking, common examples are prostitution, sexual slavery, and rape. In all these cases, what is really being discussed is sex trafficking—the most common and popular reason for human trafficking. The U.S. Department of State (2005) defines sex trafficking as the recruitment, harboring, transportation, provision, or obtaining of a person by threat or force for the commercialization of a sex act. For clarity, a commercial sex act is one in which money or property is given in exchange for sex. In earlier definitions it was the prostitute who received the benefit of the payment for performing a sexual act; however, the United Nations extended the definition of sex trafficking to include payments or benefits to a person with control over another person for the purpose of exploitation and, thus, recognized the role of the trafficker in human trafficking (McGinnis, 2004). With the passing of the 2000 Trafficking Victims Protection Act (TVPA) in the United States, sex trafficking was identified as not only a crime against humanity but also a specific violation of U.S. federal law.

Sex trafficking is not simply prostitution. It involves others in addition to the prostitute (or sex worker) and his or her client. The trafficker controls not only the sexual exploitation of his or her sex worker but is also his or her worker's movements and "choice" to work or not work with a particular client. In most of the documented cases of sex trafficking in the United States, victims are prostituted through force, fraud, or coercion on the part of their traffickers and do not have the ability to end the prostitution when they choose to begin another lifestyle. Victims of sex trafficking may be male or female; however, the majority of victims in the United States and internationally are women and underage girls. Sex trafficking is not limited to the act of prostitution; however, most cases of sex trafficking include prostitution. Victims of sex trafficking are forced into various forms of commercial sexual exploitation such as prostitution, pornography, bride trafficking, and sex tourism. The common element in all forms of sex trafficking is the total control of the trafficker over his or her victim. These victims face physical abuse, emotional abuse, health risks, and sexual coercion (Doerner & Lab, 2005). They often do not receive proper food, safe shelter, or medical attention. They are also often addicted to drugs and/or alcohol provided by their traffickers. In addition, members of the victims' families may be threatened, tortured, or killed if the victims do not participate in their sexual exploitation; thus, for a victim of sex trafficking, the abuse appears to be never ending.

> Sex trafficking includes commercial sexual exploitation through activities such as prostitution and pornography.

Every state and city in the United States has an area that is known by the public for its criminal environment. The victims of sex trafficking are found in highly visible venues such as street prostitution, massage parlors, spas, and strip clubs, and the public knows they are there; what the public generally does not know is that these victims of sex trafficking are in these areas without choice. The victims of sex trafficking are also found in less visible venues, as they may work out of "legitimate" businesses or private homes and be called to prostitute for high-powered corporate employees or government employees.

> The United States is one of the top destination countries for sex trafficking. In the United States, the states of California, New York, and Texas and the city of Las Vegas are the preferred areas for traffickers attempting to establish their businesses (May, 2006a).

It is estimated by the U.S. government that human trafficking is the third most profitable of all the illegal trafficking industries, after the trafficking of drugs and the trafficking of firearms. It lacks the historical focus by the government to end the trafficking of drugs or to reduce the flow of firearms across the country (Farr, 2004). Of course, much of human trafficking is sex trafficking.

Unfortunately, just as is the case with the trafficking of drugs, those involved in the sex trafficking of humans find the action extremely profitable, and, without law enforcement efforts to end sex trafficking, this form of trafficking is perceived as lucrative with few risks or consequences. In neither gun trafficking nor drug trafficking is there a particular word or phrase to identify the major product of the trade; however, the phrase "white slavery" is commonly used to describe the European women involved in sex trafficking in this country (de Vries, 2005). These "white slaves" are prostituted without the choice of participation and forcibly moved from city to city and from state to state for profit.

National (U.S.-born) and migrant women and children are trafficked within the borders of the United States (Raymond & Hughes, 2001). This chapter focuses on these adults, most often women, who are victims of sex trafficking, on how the sex trafficking occurs, and on the conditions that fuel sex trafficking.

For clarity of discussion within this chapter, sex trafficking is divided into two categories. The first applies to forced prostitutes, that is, individuals who do not choose to participate as prostitutes (Tiefenbrun, 2002). In some cases, these victims are kidnapped in their home countries and brought into the United States with false or no documentation and then forced to work in sexually exploitive occupations. In other cases, these individuals are sold by an acquaintance or a family member for the purpose of sex trafficking.

The second category includes those individuals (most often women) who volunteer for prostitution and agree to exchange sex for money but who often are placed in situations where they perform unanticipated, undesired, and nonconsensual sexual acts under inhumane conditions (Tiefenbrun, 2002). This category of sex trafficking victims provides the most difficulty for law enforcement and the legal system as these victims know that they intended to participate in an illegal activity and are unlikely to report their victimization for fear of being arrested. It is also this category of sex trafficking victims who are perceived by the public as "unworthy" of legal assistance as they voluntarily participated in criminal activities themselves. The public often perceives this category of sex trafficking victim in the same light as the prostitute who is beaten and robbed by his or her client. If the prostitute had not been participating in a crime, then he or she would not have been a victim.

Regardless of the category of sex trafficking, the destinations for most of the trafficked women in this country are cities with large centers of trade and commerce where there are areas with either a formal or informal sex industry (Hughes, 2001). It is within these densely populated areas that the victims of sex trafficking and their traffickers may easily blend in and function with the maximum profit to the human trafficker.

In the United States, prostitution is certainly not new; it was a common occurrence in the nineteenth century. Each year, some current-day legislator will want to debate the idea of legalizing prostitution. Historically, prostitutes solicited business on street corners (they were called "street walkers") or traveled to railroad construction sites and similar locations for business. The phrase "red light district" originated from the red signal lamps that railroad workers hung outside a prostitute's tent in case their employers needed to locate the rail workers quickly (Barkan, 2001). The term "hooker" referred to the prostitutes who provided sex for General Joseph Hooker's troops during the Civil War, and the phrase "Mayflower Madam" originates from a 1980s brothel owner in New York whose ancestors came to America on the *Mayflower* (Barrows, 1989).

Many scholars suggest that prostitution is degrading to women. Others suggest that women profit from prostitution. The difference between these perceptions of prostitution stems from whether it is assumed that the prostitutes choose his or her criminal actions. This is not the assumption in sex trafficking.

> Although it is not known how much money is made from sex trafficking in the United States, a 2005 raid of ten San Francisco massage parlors led to the confiscation of $2 million in cash (May, 2006a).

Since the collapse of the Berlin Wall, an increase in the number of victims of sex trafficking has been documented throughout the European Union and the United States (Goodey, 2004). Today, the sex industry, which was previously considered marginal, occupies a central position in the development of international capitalism, and for U.S. law enforcement the fight to end sex trafficking appears endless (Poulin, 2003). The documentation of a profitable industry provides even more support for a newly recognized criminal enterprise as more and more individuals and criminal organizations attempt to profit from sex trafficking.

> Katya left Russia after she answered an ad for a nanny in New York. When Katya landed at JFK airport, she was met by two Russian mobsters and told there was no nanny job and that she owed them the money for her flight. The mobsters took her passport and gave her the job choices of stripping in a bar in New Jersey or working in a massage parlor in Brooklyn (Wiehl,

2006). Katya worked to pay off her travel expenses and the expenses she incurred while living in the United States.

Prevalence

Bales (2004) suggests that worldwide more than 200,000 individuals are enslaved as prostitutes. Some of these individuals are trafficked into and throughout the United States. In fact, Tiefenbrun (2002) suggests that approximately 50,000 of these women are trafficked into the United States for sex work on an annual basis, and many of these individuals are moved throughout the United States to provide clients with a variety of prostitutes. Experts in the field of sex trafficking suggest that the movement of these victims may be on an individual or group basis. These movements are usually based on relationships between the traffickers and brothel operators and the need for a certain type of woman within a particular geographical area (Richard, 1999). For example, in Miami, an area with many African Americans and Hispanics, a blonde female from Russia may be profitable for her trafficker. In many cases, the traffickers house the women at staging points such as locations within New York's Chinatown until the brothel owners are ready for the women (Richard, 1999).

In addition to the movement of the victims of sex trafficking for variety, traffickers will move their victims to keep them confused about their location and therefore unable to contact someone to come for help and to avoid the victims establishing relationships with clients who may choose to "rescue" them from their abuse (Richard, 1999). The length of time a victim of sex trafficking stays in one brothel is unknown, and eventually some victims may return to a particular brothel. However, research in the movement of sex trafficking victims suggests that U.S. victims will not be assigned to one brothel for more than 309 days (Richard, 1999). The conditions surrounding the victims of prostitution and other forms of sexual victimization result in mortality rates forty times higher than the national average (Chesler, 1994). Trafficking in women for the purpose of sexual exploitation is more dangerous than trafficking in women for domestic or commercial labor as victims are exposed to serious health risks such as physical violence and sexually transmitted diseases as well as their conditions of forced labor and confinement (Sulaimanova, 2006).

The U.S. government suggests that the number of individuals sex trafficked into the United States is lower than 50,000; however, the government does recognize that sex trafficking is the most common reason for human trafficking in this country. The reality now facing the United States is that the sex industry (which previously was only marginal in the U.S. economy) now occupies a central position in the development of national and international capitalism and those engineering the sex trafficking of humans now occupy some of the highest wealth strata in foreign countries (Poulin, 2003). Also, not often recognized and sometimes not counted in cases of sex trafficking are those victims born in the United States and trafficked throughout the country without crossing national borders; thus, victims of human trafficking (including sex trafficking) are not always aliens to the country. A victim of sex trafficking in the United States may be born in the country and a citizen of the United States.

It is estimated that profits from sex trafficking may be as high as $12 billion annually, and these are expected to increase within the next few years owing to the demand of the market and the limited enforcement of anti-trafficking laws worldwide (Tiefenbrun, 2002). Hughes, in her 2001 study of sex trafficking within U.S. borders, estimates the profits at $7 billion annually and suggests that this estimate is conservative as the U.S. population increasingly engages in the sex trafficking of humans. However, as for any sort of human trafficking, sex trafficking is an activity that does not lend itself to the openness required for accuracy in reporting (Schauer & Wheaton, 2006).

How It Happens

It is impossible to document the first time in U.S. history when sex trafficking occurred; however, in the 1980s globalization and technology made the movement of victims across international borders much easier. It is known that organizations that help fight sex trafficking have only existed within the past thirty years (Guinn & Steglich, 2003). In this era of civil rights and civil liberties, it is amazing to many individuals that sex trafficking can occur and that it does occur within the United States.

In the United States, most human trafficking organizations are small units of one to five individuals who identify, transport, house, and prostitute the victims of sex trafficking (Raymond and Hughes, 2001). However, in some cases, larger criminal networks (more than fifty people) may be involved in the international to national trafficking of persons from one location to another. Although fifty individuals do not prostitute the victims, there are many public and private actors involved in the process of sex trafficking.

Therefore, the network of recruiters, transporters, and pimps may be quite large, especially when one includes those public actors providing false documents for immigration officials at country borders; those private actors (cab drivers, hotel employees, and bartenders) who provide the clients access to the victims; and the public actors (social service aids, law enforcement officers, and immigration officials) who ignore the criminal activity (Guinn & Steglich, 2003).

In considering these international individuals transported within the United States, Somerset (2004) suggested that both women and children are trafficked throughout Europe and into either Canada or the United States via Heathrow and Gatwick airports in London or from England, through Scotland, into Canada, and into the United States. Of course, as with any established route of trafficking, once law enforcement has identified the specific city-to-city movements of victims, the traffickers alter the route.

In support of a general trend of human trafficking routes into the United States, Raymond and Hughes (2001) report U.S. points of entry and strategic sites along the Unites States/Canada and United States/Mexico borders and at international airports. Thus, the trafficking of an international victim into the United States involves very specific individuals whose specialties are creating false documentation and establishing relationships with others involved in the criminal network, individuals employed by the transportation authorities with the ability not to report abnormalities, and individuals involved in immigration with the power of discretion. In addition, for the trafficking of individuals born in the United States and trafficked within the United States, unless the victim reports the abuse or a law enforcement officer discovers the case, those victims are essentially undetectable and easily moved by car, plane, and so on throughout the country. In either case—U.S. native or nonnative—once the victim of sex trafficking successfully enters the United States, he or she is essentially undetectable unless law enforcement agencies are alerted to a specific case.

In attempting to explain how sex trafficking can occur, the explanation can be traced to the founding ideas of Lee's (1966) push–pull theory of migration. Specifically, just as with immigration in general, there are characteristics of a host country that push its natives out and conditions of the destination country that pull the immigrants in. Most explanations for how human trafficking can occur focus on the conditions of the host areas. One common method of recruiting women for sex trafficking is by placing an advertisement in local newspapers for nannies or waitresses in the United States. Once the women have been recruited, they are transported to the United States, where their travel documents are confiscated and they are imprisoned by their traffickers and forced to pay off their "debts," which include the costs of their transportation, food, clothing, and shelter (Bell, 2001).

Farr (2004) suggests that in areas with a strong military presence, there is often poverty and unemployment, which leads to many women being employed as prostitutes. In fact, the association between sex trafficking and the U.S. military was recognized as early as the Vietnam War, when even U.S. military bases were flooded with international girls working as prostitutes. Large numbers of Asian prostitutes were trafficked to the Fayetteville, North Carolina, base (whose nickname was Fayettnam) to serve the soldiers (McGinnis, 2004).

This prostitution on military bases provides the need of destination countries for sex trafficking. The prostitution, such as the activity in Fayettnam in the United States, serves both the military and the prostitutes well while the members of the military are stationed in the area, as the strong customer base provides a demand for the prostitute. Unfortunately, when the military vacates the area, that demand for prostitutes no longer exists; therefore, the prostitutes remain in the area without work. The women employed as prostitutes to serve the soldiers during the occupation are now not profitable, and it is these women who become the prime targets for those interested in victims for sex trafficking.

> In countries of origin, characteristics such as poverty, unemployment, war, and oppression are all associated with fueling the market for sex trafficking.

It is not unusual for women employed as prostitutes to serve a military base to be sent elsewhere once the military units leave the area. Many of these individuals who have chosen prostitution in the area will choose to relocate for prostitution. Zimmerman (2003) reports that most sex-trafficked adults are simply aged prostitutes and that many choose to relocate for prostitution; however, few realize the captivity involved in sex trafficking. Thus, again we have the problem of women who initially agree to move to an area (or country) with the intention to work in that area as a prostitute or in another avenue of the sex industry being an easy target for a sex trafficker attempting to increase his or her profits. These women will resist contacting the authorities for fear of being arrested and, in the case of those born outside the United States, for fear of being sent back to a country where they cannot secure work.

Another explanation for sex trafficking suggests that human slavery thrives on extreme poverty (Bales, 2004). This is especially true for victims of inequality. In particular, women are seen as a liability in some families and these women will often volunteer to be trafficked for sex work (Raymond & Hughes, 2001). Given conditions of poverty and extreme oppression, the trafficking of humans is considered a great source of revenue for many (victims included). In some cases, women who contract with pimps or traffickers for the cost of their transportation are sold from one pimp to another. Each time this happens, the debt to her current pimp starts all over and the woman has essentially sold herself into slavery (Hughes, 2001). Even women who enter the sex industry as strippers will, in most cases, eventually begin prostitution as a victim of sex trafficking and thus further sexual exploitation.

Another underreported and often unacknowledged source of human trafficking is the family of the victim. Just as the family often perpetrates child abuse (McCabe, 2003), the family, entrusted to love and protect, will allow its members, in particular young women, to be trafficked for sex. Hotaling and Finkelhor (1988) suggest that family members introduce prostitutes to sexual exploitation at a very early age (childhood) and that these individuals are raised in an environment of sexual exploitation; hence, it is not surprising that they become victims of sexual exploitation outside of their hometown or native country. In these cases of human trafficking for sexual exploitation, victims volunteer or are sold or traded by their families (Farr, 2004).

One day a young woman may be in the company of her family. The next day she may be prostituted by her father. The next month she may be sold by her family and trafficked outside of her home for further prostitution. Such young women are trapped by their traffickers. They cannot return to their families as their fathers or brothers have sold them. Thus they continue to work for fear of punishment inflicted on their family by the traffickers or fear of punishment by their family members who agreed to and profited by their entry into sex trafficking. As with many U.S. prostitutes, victims of sex trafficking are likely to be victims of a sexually abusive family member.

To increase the likelihood of exploitation, those involved in the day-to-day operations of the mail-order bride business may also be instigators of sex trafficking. Cullen (2002) reports that mail-order brides often become trapped in an environment of slavery and prostitution. A young woman who wishes to leave the poverty and inequality of her home country may choose to become a mail-order bride to an American man. American men are increasingly using international matchmaking agencies or mail-order bride catalogs to find a spouse. Unfortunately, though these are considered legitimate businesses, they are essentially unregulated, with neither the brides nor the grooms screened for criminal histories. In 1999, Immigration and Naturalization Services (INS) reported that there were more than 200 mail-order bride agencies operating in the United States and that between 4,000 and 6,000 women were entering the country each year as potential brides. Unfortunately for these victims, the love and security of a home are not the outcomes. In fact, these women are often perceived as disposable or replaceable by their new husbands. Mail-order bride brokers are not considered traffickers, but they are regarded as frauds in not disclosing all the facts. These brokers may be liable as traffickers (Miller and Stewart, 1998). The brides who enter the United States for marriage may end up as slaves.

Spousal prostitution is also related to sex trafficking. McCabe's (2007a) phrase "spousal prostitution" describes the phenomenon of husbands receiving money from individuals in exchange for sex with the husband's wife. In this organized prostitution, the husband could serve as the pimp for his wife or the wife, lacking the labor skills or education for a profitable occupation within the United States, must engage in prostitution to earn money for her husband's household. Of course, this is not the situation assumed to exist by the young women who agree to become mail-order brides; however, some mail-order brides do become victims of spousal prostitution. In addition, some victims of spousal prostitution are forced to participate in sexual activities by their husbands and moved throughout the country (against their will) to avoid detection and to provide the financial means of survival for their husbands. These victims of spousal prostitution are also victims of sex trafficking. In countries of origin, characteristics such as poverty, unemployment, war, and oppression are all associated with fueling the market for sex trafficking.

> Sex trafficking may involve spousal prostitution. Spousal prostitution most often involves the husband receiving money or drugs in exchange for allowing another individual to have sex with his wife (McCabe, 2007a).

The link between prostitution and sex trafficking is always an aspect to consider when attempting to explain sex trafficking (U.S. Department of State, 2004a). In addition, sex tours and sex rings are often involved with sex trafficking (Brown, 1999). For clarity, McCabe (2003) uses the phrase "sex ring" to describe a situation in which two or more offenders are simultaneously involved in the sexual exploitation of several victims. The phrase "sex tour" entails the rotation of victims through geographic locations for sexual exploitation.

Sex rings and sex tours are both related to sex trafficking in that victims, for this discussion adult woman, are rotated or passed from abuser to abuser; thus, they are victimized repeatedly without the option to end the sexual exploitation.

The United States has historically taken a firm stand against the legalization of prostitution not only because it is demeaning to women but also because it directly contributes to the modern-day slave trade (U.S. Department of States, 2004b). Legalized prostitution and its related activities fuel sex trafficking in that these legitimate businesses serve as fronts for those traffickers targeting individuals for sexual exploitation (Hughes, Carlson, & Carlson, 2002). In areas where prostitution is legal, such as in the eleven counties of Nevada, the cost of sexual services includes the cost of rent, medical examinations, and so on. Therefore, many individuals will attempt to satisfy the market demand for cheaper prostitutes and participate in illegal prostitution within the areas of legal prostitution to reduce the costs to the clients and increase profits for the pimps.

Legalized prostitution is a trafficker's best shield from law enforcement in that it allows him or her to "legitimize" his or her slave trade by making it difficult to distinguishing the victims of sex trafficking from legal prostitutes. In other words, in areas such as Las Vegas, known for legalized prostitution, victims of sex trafficking are blended into the daily activities of the legal sex trade and thus are difficult to identify among the thousands of legal prostitutes. To further assist the trafficking victims to blend into the world of legalized prostitution, many of the brothel owners establish a customer base of their own nationality to help ensure confidentiality. In other words, for example, Mexican brothel owners will permit only other Mexicans into their businesses; thus, the trafficking victims are unknown to those customers outside of the Mexican community (Richard, 1999).

Emerging entrepreneurs in the area of sexual exploitation are those who utilize film and the Internet. This is the newest avenue for victims of sex trafficking, as often the perpetrators of sex trafficking will "employ" individuals in video production depicting the sexual exploitation of individuals (Taylor & Jamieson, 1999). Of course, these victims receive little or no compensation. Although it is illegal to distribute many of their pornographic and sadistic films over the Internet, law enforcement and Internet service providers (ISPs) rarely monitor these activities, and unless an illegal activity is discovered through a screen by the ISP or a report to law enforcement, the activity continues. Thus, the distribution of images of sexual exploitation and the use of the victims of sex trafficking to produce the images found on the Internet essentially are allowed to flow freely (McCabe, 2007b). In a nutshell, Tiefenbrun (2002) suggests that sex trafficking in the United States has increased owing to conditions in the countries of origin, the limited domestic laws, the weak international treaties, and the demand for sexual exploitation in the United States. Regardless of the reasons, the number of documented cases of sex trafficking in the United States has increased.

Victims

In considering the victims of sex trafficking, the U.S. Department of State (2004a) reports that at least 70% of the women trafficked and at least 50% of the children trafficked across the world are trafficked for sexual exploitation. Of these victims many are either European or Asian and many are victims of sex trafficking within the borders of the United States. However, the primary source countries for sex trafficking into the United States are Thailand, Vietnam, China, Mexico, Russia, the Ukraine, and the Czech Republic (Richard, 1999). There have also been cases of sex trafficking victims coming to the United States from the Philippines, Korea, Malaysia, Hungary, Poland, Brazil, and Honduras. The general demographic characteristics of the victims of sex trafficking are, of course, young and female. In that sexual exploitation is the commodity of trade, the more "attractive" the product, the higher the sale price. Although specifics on the ages of those trafficked for sex are unknown, it is suggested that the average age of a sex slave outside of the United States is just eleven years and around twenty in the United States (Wiehl, 2006). Ideal for the situation of sex trafficking is that many of the victims are not only young and female but also have very little English proficiency. The lack of ability to speak in English is a critical element in many of the cases of sex trafficking in the United States, as victims, once they express to their traffickers the desire to end the sexual exploitation, are often unable because of language barriers to report their abuse to U.S. law enforcement or social services officials.

Given that many of the victims of sex trafficking have had experience with government officials whose own corruption has supported their victimization, that they do not possess what we would consider marketable skills for employment, and that they are not proficient in English and thus are not able to provide detailed accounts of the sex trafficking, the victims of sex trafficking feel they must depend on their traffickers for their survival and will not report the abuse. This "code of silence" among the victims of sex trafficking (similar to that of domestic violence victims) often remains in place even when the victims are questioned by law enforcement about their victimization.

Raymond and Hughes (2001), in their description of women trafficked from what was once the Soviet Union, reported that most of the women entered the sex business at an early age, most were employed in the sex industry before they entered the United States, few could speak English, and most either entered the United States on a tourist visa or were trafficked on fraudulent papers. In addition to the abuse encountered by victims of sex trafficking, these individuals often face numerous health risks from unprotected sex alone, as many victims will have sex with ten to twenty men per day, putting them at risk for unwanted pregnancies and at-home abortions, HIV, and other sexually transmitted diseases. To further compound the risk of HIV and AIDS among victims of sex trafficking, it is also not unheard of for traffickers to purchase HIV-positive females at little cost and then place them in the rotation for sex trafficking. These HIV-positive victims are rotated in and out of areas quickly; therefore, they are impossible to contact for HIV testing, follow-up testing, or for identification in new cases of HIV. These HIV-positive victims are cheap, disposable, and extremely profitable for their traffickers.

In considering the case of Asian women trafficked for sexual exploitation within the United States, the description of those individuals, once again, mirrors that of the Eastern European women; however, the difference with many of the original Asian victims of sex trafficking was the fact that these Asian women entered the United States as wives of military personnel and were later prostituted. Again, without a command of the English language, these victims of sex trafficking were unable to seek assistance to end their abuse. Without communication skills, the majority of their encounters with law enforcement resulted in either arrest or deportation.

North America, and in particular the United States, is the most reported destination region for sex trafficking (Kangaspunta, 2006). Whether this phenomenon is a result of spousal prostitution, of a decision to seek employment in the United States, or of the mail-order bride industry, the victims of sex trafficking are transported (or smuggled) to the United States and throughout the country for the purpose of sexual activity. Without the English skills to request help from law enforcement or social services, and with the fear of U.S. authorities instilled in them by either their captors or their home country, they are captives and forced to participate in sexual exploitation throughout the country; hence, they are trafficked for sex without an avenue for escape.

Offenders

In considering the offenders in sex trafficking, one must consider two distinct categories. The first includes those offenders (or traffickers) who make available human beings for sex trafficking—the individuals who recruit (or kidnap) the victims, the individuals who transport those victims to and throughout the United States, and the individuals who foster the sexual abuse of the victims. The second category comprises the customers who pay to abuse the victims. In this category, discussions of offenders must acknowledge their rationale to participate in and pay for sexual exploitation. In a nutshell, the traffickers themselves enter the sex trafficking business for profit and the customers enter the business for a service. Unfortunately, as for most of the research on prostitution, in the area of sex trafficking, little research exists on anyone other than the victim involved or abused in the sex trafficking, and much of that information is based on very small samples (Raymond, 2004).

This lack of offender information, for the most part, is explained by the secrecy of this activity. In the United States, the sex trafficking of women is primarily accomplished through crime rings and criminal networks. Some of these crime rings are exclusively involved in human trafficking and some are involved in a number of diversified criminal activities (Kangaspunta, 2006).

Those involved exclusively in human trafficking are more likely to be organized around a core group (Kangaspunta, 2006). In this organizational structure, a small number of individuals form a relatively tight and structure core group. Around this small core is a larger group of associated individuals, and around this group of associated individuals is a larger number of peripheral players.

In terms of the organizational structure of criminal networks involving diversified criminal activities, a hierarchically structured organization exists and is characterized by distinct lines of control and responsibility (Kangaspunta, 2006). In this organizational structure, there exists a single leadership structure and a strong sense of identity and responsibilities in terms of criminal actions (see Figure 1).

Regardless of the structure, there are large, medium, and small criminal networks involved in the sex trafficking of women (Bertone, 2000). Specifically, large-scale networks recruit women in what appear to be legal ways, such as posing as employment agency employees with national and international contacts to identify nannies for work in the United States. The medium-scale networks, thought most often to exist for entry into the United States, traffic women from country to country, and the small-scale organized crime networks

Criminal Organizational Structures

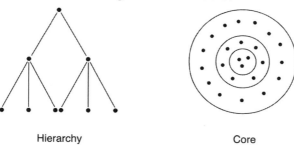

Hierarchy   Core

traffic women on the basis of requests for certain types of women from brothel owners (Bertone, 2000).

Those involved in sex trafficking work under the same models as drug trafficking or weapons trafficking. Individuals involved in sex trafficking are often identified only through gatekeepers in the industry. Those involved in the trafficking of individuals for sex guard themselves against authorities in immigration, in law enforcement, and in social services. The network of traffickers is quite often small and the leaking of information is unlikely. In larger networks for sex trafficking, members of the organization rarely know all of the players; hence, identification of a large number of specific individuals is unlikely. In fact, in large organizations for sex trafficking, individual members may know only one or two other members (only those with whom they have direct contact); therefore, identification of all of the offenders is impossible. In these conditions, and given the fact that traffickers will resort to extreme violence in controlling their workers and the information obtained through those workers, it is difficult to identify the actual participants within the criminal network (Hughes, 2001).

Sex traffickers attract their victims from the poverty of their homes with promises of employment, marriage, or an education. The victims are then forced into prostitution (McGinnis, 2004).

Bales (2004) suggests that another identifying characteristic of traffickers is that those involved in trafficking are often "respectable" businesspeople who own brothels through investment clubs. The identity of such traffickers is often hidden under the red tape of legitimate business bureaucracy. As the profit from illegal sex trafficking may be hidden in the legitimate profits reported to the Internal Revenue Service (IRS) and as criminal laws have little deterrent effect, the IRS and the U.S. Senate Finance Committee have proposed new tax laws that essentially identify pimps as employers and their prostitutes as employees for taxation purposes (CBSNews.com, 2006). The profit-making potential in sex trafficking far outweighs that in smuggling. In particular, often the first thing a smuggled immigrant will do, once he or she reaches the country of destination, is call his or her family. This is an indication of successful transport and the signal that the smuggling fee should be paid (Chin, 1999). The relationship between the smuggler and client has ended. Victims of sex trafficking are generally not allowed to call home; thus, their time and profit for their trafficker is not over (Chin, 1999).

Once a woman is purchased for sex trafficking, a trafficker can make five to twenty times her purchase price (Hughes, 2001). By requiring a tax on the victim's profit to the trafficker, additional ways to penalize sex traffickers are established. In light of this assertion of financial gain with little or no chance of penalty, it is naive to predict that more "legitimate" business owners will not enter into the word of sex trafficking.

To provide some general characteristics of traffickers, most research supports the notion that the majority of these individuals are male; however, it must be acknowledged that women, often in the role of a brothel madam, are also involved in the day-to-day schedules of a trafficked woman and in some cases are becoming more actively involved in the process. In many cases, women actually target and recruit other young women to enter the business (May, 2006b). Many of the traffickers share the nationality of the victims of sex trafficking, and most of the victims are recruited by persons known to them (Kangaspunta, 2006). This causes even more difficulty in identifying the perpetrators of sex trafficking. Also acknowledged is that, in many cases, those responsible for the trafficking and the sexual exploitation are the husbands of the victims (McCabe, 2007a).

One of the best ways to identify the perpetrators of sex trafficking is to identify the environment of sex trafficking. Specifically, areas prone to sex trafficking are areas with heavy security around establishments, including bars on the windows and strong locks on the doors (Miller, 2006). Victims of sex trafficking are rarely (if ever) seen leaving the premises without an escort (or translator) as the victims of sex trafficking often live and work at the same premises.

Finally, in terms of the characteristics of the clients of sex-trafficked women, Raymond and Hughes (2001) report that solicitors are of all ages and all socioeconomic statuses. In addition, the clients of sex-trafficked women often expect unprotected sex and the ability to subject their victims to physical violence or humiliation if they so desire. Again, without a clear description of these offenders, any sort of profiling is impossible and law enforcement is forced to respond to sex trafficking only through a reactive mode based on reports of sexual exploitation and abuse and is thus unable proactively to put an end to the abuse by the targeting or profiling of offenders involved in sex trafficking.

> Kika came from Venezuela through an invitation from an American man offering her love and friendship. Her boyfriend took her passport and money and then forced her to work in a brothel with other enslaved girls. She was victimized for three years before she was discovered (Wiehl, 2006).

Fueling the Problem

As with any sort of illegal activity, there are always multiple explanations for the phenomenon. The sex trafficking of individuals is not unique in this respect. Sex trafficking is a multibillion-dollar industry that has what seems to be an endless supply of women ready to be used for profit (Farr, 2004). In countries of economic depression where women are seen as disposable, victims of sex trafficking are replaced on a daily basis. Sex tours are offered by some disreputable travel industries (Mirkinson, 1997) and consumers in the United States want, and will pay for, exotic bodies from other countries (Poulin, 2003).

One example was a case filed against New York's Big Apple Oriental Tours for promoting sexual exploitation and human trafficking. If we add the fact that many countries have very relaxed immigration laws and allow individuals to move from destination to destination without proper documentation (Tiefenbrun, 2002), it is no wonder that the U.S. law enforcement agencies are now experiencing their share of sex trafficking cases. Again, with supply available and with constant demand in the United States, cases of sex trafficking are expected to continue and, without strong laws and enforcement of these laws, perhaps increase, because many of the current laws have been enacted without clarity of terms such as "consent" and the difference between "smuggling" and "trafficking" (Doezema, 2005).

Investigative challenge is another aspect fueling the problem of sex trafficking in the United States. Not only are resources limited for law enforcement, but they are also limited for prosecutors, and with little experience in the area of sex trafficking, many prosecutors will attempt to settle cases through pleas instead of trials. Finally, as discussed, law enforcement officials rarely receive a report of sex trafficking, and many are unable to distinguish these cases from cases of prostitution; therefore, without the recognition of victims and the victims' willingness to report, sex trafficking continues.

Limited penalties for sex traffickers are another reason to expect increases in sex trafficking in the United States. In comparing a case of human trafficking with a case of drug trafficking, the maximum sentence for slavery is perhaps ten years whereas distributing a kilo of heroin could mean a life sentence (Richard, 1999).

Finally, many of the women who are victims of sex trafficking in the United States did not enter the country legally. Unfortunately, it has been the case that these women were often penalized by immigration officials and removed from the country rather than assisted by social services (Tiefenbrun, 2002). The TVPA provided a shift in this practice as victims of sex trafficking are now offered a T visa, which gives them temporary resident status in this country, as it is recognized that deportation could mean death for the victims and their families. Through the T visa, victims may apply for permanent resident status after three years, and, in some cases, this status may be applied to their family members.

> The Internet now provides another avenue for recruiting, advertising for, and identifying victims of sex trafficking (McCabe, 2007b).

One cannot also underestimate the impact of the Internet in the transnational and national trafficking of people for sexual exploitation, as it is not uncommon for traffickers to be found with filming equipment and computers to create and sell pornography (McGinnis, 2004). Researchers are just beginning to recognize the role played by the World Wide Web in the covert or overt advertising of specific sexual services as there exists few systematic approaches to investigating the specific Internet marketplaces of this new cyber-trade (Taylor & Jamieson, 1999).

Many police and governmental organizations are now focusing on the Internet, the World Wide Web, and digital television to identify and pursue cases of sex trafficking (Taylor & Jamieson, 1999). However, with limited law enforcement resources and training to address the Internet and its multiple avenues into criminal activity (McCabe, 2007b), cases of sex trafficking via the Internet are also expected to continue, and the number is expected to increase at a much faster rate than the number of law enforcement or governmental regulatory agencies.

Researchers such as Sulaimanova (2006) suggest that countries of origin can reduce sex trafficking by fostering environments that create legitimate employment opportunities for women, providing legal and medical assistance to victims, and focusing governmental efforts to reduce the official corruption often involved in human trafficking. Destination countries can support anti-trafficking legislation in terms of law enforcement training and efforts, provide assistance to victims, punish those involved as clients to sex-trafficked victims, and maximize prison sentences for those convicted of sex trafficking.

The United States is among the top three destinations for sex traffickers globally. Women are trafficked into the sex industry of the United States with promises of lucrative jobs only to be sold into brothels or to strip clubs (May, 2006a). Along with Japan and Australia, the United States is the land of opportunity and victimization for those exploited through sex trafficking.

Summary

Sex trafficking is the recruitment, harboring, transportation, provision, or obtaining of a person by threat or force for the commercialization of a sex act. Under the TVPA, sex trafficking is a federal crime. Sex trafficking is divided into two categories. The first is forced prostitution and the second includes those individuals (most often women) who volunteer for prostitution and agree to exchange sex for money but who often are later placed in situations that result in their performing nonconsensual sexual acts without the ability to end their abuse.

In the United States, the top destinations for sex trafficking are California, New York, Texas, and Las Vegas. The primary source countries for sex trafficking into the United States are Thailand, Vietnam, China, Mexico, Russia, the Ukraine, and the Czech Republic. In most of the documented cases of sex trafficking in the United States, victims are prostituted through force, fraud, or coercion on the part of their traffickers.

Sex trafficking is the result of the conditions of a country of origin as well as the conditions of the country of destination. Specifically, extreme poverty and oppression of women in a country may encourage residents to leave in search of a better life and for an income for their families. Countries with residents who have an existing desire for individuals employed in the sex industry may welcome the victims of sex trafficking for exploitation.

Both men and women are involved in the trafficking of humans for sexual exploitation. Most research supports the idea that the majority of the traffickers are male; however, researchers may soon change their conclusions about the gender of offenders, as more and more women are becoming involved as recruiters, transporters, or brothel madams.

Critical in the definition of sex trafficking is that it occurs without the consent of the victim. In addition, the victims of sex trafficking often do not possess the language skills or the trust in U.S. law enforcement required to help them if they decide to end the exploitation. Without the ability to end the abuse, many victims of sex trafficking continue to suffer until they die or are killed.

Finally, sex trafficking is a profitable enterprise, with estimates of annual profits in the millions of dollars. This profit from sex trafficking has historically come with very few negative consequences if it is discovered by law enforcement; hence, for all involved, sex trafficking appears to be a phenomenon that will only increase in the United States.

Questions on Chapter 2

1. How is sex trafficking defined? How is this definition different from that of human trafficking?
2. What are the two major categories of sex trafficking? Why is the distinction between the two important?
3. Why is it difficult to obtain exact numbers on the incidence and prevalence of cases of sex trafficking?
4. How are victims of sex trafficking recruited or identified? Why does the method of recruitment matter?
5. Why is it felt that, in the United States, cases of sex trafficking will continue to increase in number?

Questions for Further Thought

1. Why is sex trafficking the commonest form of human trafficking?
2. If individuals agree to prostitute themselves in exchange for their transportation fee into the United Sates, are they still victims if they later decide not to participate in prostitution but are forced to continue?

3. If geographical areas of vulnerability for the entry of people for sex trafficking into the United States have been identified, why is there still a problem?
4. Why is the United States an attractive destination for sex trafficking?
5. What can the United States do to reduce the pull it has for the industry of sex trafficking?

· 3 ·

LABOR TRAFFICKING

According to the International Labour Office (2005), at least twelve million people are trapped in forced labor today. Of those, more than two million are victims of human trafficking. There are several reasons for human trafficking other than sexual exploitation; one of those is labor. Labor trafficking, in itself, is profitable. As trafficked individuals generate millions of dollars each year in profit for their traffickers, with annual estimates of approximately $13,000 per trafficked laborer, it is doubtful that those involved in human trafficking will simply decide to cease the criminal activity. It is this type of human trafficking that is just beginning to receive legislative attention.

Unfortunately, for those interested in labor trafficking, little in terms of empirical research exists beyond the topic of sex trafficking (Munro, 2006). For many years, the phrase "human trafficking" was used to describe sex trafficking. Labor trafficking was not viewed as a major problem in many countries, and as identifying the victims of forced labor was even less fruitful than identifying the victims of sex trafficking, it was not studied and it did not receive focused attention from law enforcement officials (Kangaspunta, 2006). In only the most recent years, and to comply with the definition of the UN's Trafficking Protocol, legislation has been adopted to include the actions of labor trafficking. Today, the conditions of forced labor and labor trafficking are recognized, but not to the same extent as those of sex trafficking.

In 2006, Doyle suggested that at least one million people worldwide were subjected to some form of forced labor trafficking. People forced into labor may be found in the fields, in meat packing plants, in canneries, in sweatshops, as maids, as nannies, and in restaurant and custodial work (Miller, 2006). Victims of labor trafficking are often "hidden" in plain sight of legitimate jobs; therefore, there is no reason to suspect illegal activity. In addition, victims of forced labor, especially those victims in industry, are so "out of reach" of upper management and inspection officers that they are never seen; thus, the victimization continues without suspicion.

In the United States, in addition to sex trafficking, human trafficking for labor is quickly becoming a concern as newspaper headlines detailing the abuse of laborers in the sweatshops of New York or on the farms of California bring the issue of forced labor to the front page for public consumption. This concern has led states such as South Carolina to pass legislation (H.3060, Act 266) which identifies persons who knowingly force another person into labor or services as guilty of a felony known as trafficking in persons for forced labor or services. Upon conviction, these traffickers must be imprisoned for not more than fifteen years. Iowa has passed legislation (SF 2219) with penalties of a minimum of twenty-five years in prison for those found guilty of labor trafficking (OCD, 2006). This chapter is dedicated to a discussion of labor trafficking as it applies to adults worldwide.

For clarity, in this chapter, labor trafficking is defined as the recruitment, harboring, transportation, provision, or obtaining of a person for labor or services, through the use of force, fraud, or coercion for the purpose of subjection to involuntary servitude, peonage, debt bondage, or slavery (U.S. Department of State, 2004a). Labor trafficking, as defined by the U.S. Department of Health and Human Services (2005), includes not only bonded labor and forced labor but also child labor. Although children are trafficked for labor on a daily basis, given the secrecy of child trafficking overall, it is nearly impossible to gain specific information on child labor cases unless they become known to the courts. It is, however, known that in those cases of trafficking for child labor, traffickers typically bring a child to the country with the claim that the child is their niece or nephew, and then the child is forced to work long hours under unhealthy and often dangerous conditions (Richard, 1999). As Chapter 5 is dedicated to a discussion of child trafficking, this chapter discusses bonded and forced labor as it applies only to adult men and women. Interesting is the fact that whereas sex trafficking is almost exclusively limited to women and young girls (at least as reflected in police reports), labor trafficking includes both males and females as victims. In fact, where sources explicitly report the exploitation of males, the highest rates of male victims are in labor trafficking in the United States (Kangaspunta, 2006). Despite the lack of information or research focusing on labor trafficking, it is a significant part of human trafficking that existed even before the establishment of the United States and, in many ways, helped to form the United States and build it into the country it is today.

United States v. Manusurangkun (1996)

Approximately seventy-five Thai laborers were brought to California with promises of high wages and freedom. Once they arrived, they were forced into twenty-hour shifts of labor at a garment factory. These Thai nationals were abused and imprisoned within the factory and made to pay indentured servitude debts of thousands of dollars. Their abusers were convicted of alien smuggling, involuntary servitude, and civil rights violations. The convicted offenders received sentences ranging from seven months to seven years.

Bonded labor and forced labor are two forms of involuntary servitude related to labor trafficking. Bonded labor (also called debt bondage), although the least familiar form of labor trafficking, is a means through which victims pay off loans—often for transportation expenses into the United States—with their labor (U.S. Department of Health and Human Services, 2005). Forced labor, the better known reason for labor trafficking, is a term for work relations in which victims are forced to work against their will, under threats of violence, or when their freedom of movement is restricted.

Involuntary servitude involves servitude by means of any scheme or plan that causes a person to believe that failure to perform as conditioned will result in physical harm or the threat of the legal system (U.S. Department of State, 2004b).

Bonded Labor

The United States was built, and progressed quickly during the time of the Industrial Revolution, on bonded labor. Immigrants, in exchange for their passage to the new world and for the opportunity to learn a trade, would work (often under the title of an apprentice) for seven or so years for a craftsman before beginning to practice their own profession. The same arrangement was made for children (most often boys) in their preteens as they too worked for a craftsman to learn the trade before starting out on their own.

An indentured servant is a bonded laborer who, through a contract with their employer, works for a specific amount of time (usually seven to eight years) to reimburse their employer for their passage to a new country or location. In most instances of indentured servitude, the employer pays little in terms of monetary compensation; however, they do provide accommodation, food, and job training (if required). The phrase "bonded labor" refers to this type of indentured servitude. In cases in which bonded laborers are not provided the environment for learning and care, human and civil rights are often violated. Specifically, there are cases of bonded labor in which employers create a climate of fear to hold workers in conditions of servitude and forced labor. These "employees" become trafficked victims through their employers' use of deception, including the fraudulent misrepresentation of the transportation, employment, and conditions around their work environments (HRW, 2006). Thus, bonded labor is one of the least known forms of labor trafficking today.

In the United States, the Department of State (2004b) reports that people forced into indentured servitude can be found regularly in sweatshops, fields, domestic situations, construction sites, and in restaurants and custodial work. In some texts, bonded labor is referred to as debt bondage as victims are bonded (in much the same way as in historical accounts of apprenticeships) and their labor is used as a means of repayment of a loan. Bonded labor is criminalized under U.S. federal law and included as a type of exploitation in the United Nations Protocol on Human Trafficking (U.S. Department of State, 2005).

> In 2003 a jury in Hawaii convicted the owner of a garment factory of enslaving hundreds of workers. These workers, who often slept two to a bed, were not only held against their will but also beaten by guards (CNN. com, 2003).

In the building of the United States, much of the labor was bonded labor; anywhere from 50% to 75% of all the white immigrants to colonial America arrived as indentured servants (Galson, 1981). Under this arrangement, the servant would sell himself or herself to a ship captain who, in turn, would sell the individual to an employer once they reached their destination (Kolchin, 1993). In theory, the servant sold only his or her labor; however, in practice it may have been different. In fact, after many cases of abuse by employers, courts began recognizing the problems associated with bonded labor and began requiring documentation to support all immigration in the 1800s. The documentation to support entry into the United States is still in place and, after September 11, is more strictly enforced. However, once individuals enter the United States, their treatment by their employers was often considered "personal" or a family matter.

Today, in some cases of bonded labor, there is still abuse as victims are monitored around the clock and charged inflated rent for substandard housing (Lush, 2004). Most often, in cases of bringing the individual into the country without the proper travel documentation, or trafficking, a reasonable assessment of the victim's labor is not utilized in determining their salary nor are adequate housing or food allowances determined; hence, the trafficked bonded laborers are forced to work for even longer periods of time to "repay" the debt they owe their employers.

Unique to the bonded labor of trafficked victims is that this "debt" that they must repay is incurred from the expenses of transportation to the United States, the expenses of transportation to their workplace, and the expenses related to their food and shelter while they are in servitude. Thus, the trafficked bonded laborer must work to repay not only the expenses (including the cost of false documentation) related to entering the United States, such as transportation and bribes to border officials, but also the expenses required to work in the United States.

> Examples of U.S. cases of labor trafficking include agriculture, factory work, domestic servitude, construction, food service, and transportation of drugs.

Forced Labor

Quite often the defense for perpetrators of human trafficking for labor relies on the fact that individuals choose to sell their labor in exchange for passage into the country. Unfortunately, these bonded laborers are not seen by the public as victims when the conditions of their employment are not ideal. This is not the case with trafficked forced laborers. The phrase "forced labor" refers to the situation in which individuals are forced, under the threat of violence, deportation, or some other form of punishment, to work against their will. Domestic workers in the United States whose labor conditions constitute servitude or forced labor are often victims of labor trafficking (HRW, 2006).

In 2002, Florida courts convicted three citrus contractors for harboring hundreds of undocumented workers, for threatening these workers with violence, and for holding them hostage over financial debts (CNN.com, 2003).

Forced labor can also involve harvesting crops, with workers relocated according to the seasonality of the produce, or manufacturing plants, with more than forty hours of work expected on a weekly basis. The key components in establishing cases of forced labor are the elements of control and threats of violence by the employer and a lack of free will on the part of the victim. Victims of forced labor live a life marked by abuse, fear, and violation of basic human rights. In addition, these individuals are rarely in their native countries; therefore, they face other obstacles such as isolation from their family and friends and, often, language barriers.

In cases of human trafficking for forced labor, the victims are unable to seek help from the authorities because of constant surveillance and isolation by the employers, distrust in the authorities in their countries of origin, and/or the inability to communicate precisely in English. Thus, the victims of labor trafficking perceive themselves as powerless in their own worlds. Labor trafficking is much less likely to be detected than sex trafficking. The victims of sex trafficking are usually discovered within a year or two, whereas the victims of labor trafficking (especially those victims in domestic servitude) may be victimized for four or more years before being detected.

United States v. Bradley and O'Dell (New Hampshire) (18 U.S.C. § 1589)

Two U.S. citizens were convicted on grounds of forced labor and wire fraud as they trafficked Jamaican citizens for forced labor, confiscated their passports, and forced them to live in sheds located on the property of the business in New Hampshire.

Currently in the United States, domestic work (in homes and hotels) is a prime area for labor trafficking (Lush, 2004), with children and adults vulnerable to the domestic servitude that occurs in private homes (U.S. Department of State, 2005). In addition, recent research into the mail-order bride industry suggests that it too may be associated with forced domestic labor (Crandall et al., 2005).

What many individuals do not realize is that forced labor may include not only prostitution (which receives the classification of sex trafficking) but also domestic servitude, agricultural labor, sweatshop factory labor, custodial services, food service, and begging. In fact, the Center for Immigration Studies (CIS) (2001) reports that approximately 20% of all illegal immigrants are employed as agricultural or fishing laborers, in contrast to approximately 10% of the legal immigrants. In addition, approximately 18% of illegal immigrants (particularly men) are employed in construction and 16% are employed in retail production as an operator, fabricator, or in machinery repair.

Finally, although there exist some significant differences in the employment areas of legal and illegal immigrants, there are also similarities. Specifically, immigrants (both legal and illegal) are found in areas of manufacturing, retail sales, and personal services (CIS, 2001). In the United States, as discussed in Appendix B, the majority of these immigrants are from Mexico.

Although Americans are aware of the existence of industries such as the garment businesses in the northeast or the chicken-packing plants in the southeast, they may be unaware of the fact that the non-English-speaking immigrants who produce the goods for these companies may be trafficked victims of forced labor. The same applies also to those hotel maids, apple pickers, and ethnic restaurant workers unable to communicate with their patrons in English.

Victims

The victims of labor trafficking have many commonalities with the victims of sex trafficking; however, more men are victims of labor trafficking than of sex trafficking. Among the major problems in identifying male victims are legislative limitations (Kangaspunta, 2006). Similar to the historical situation of reporting rapes in America, in many U.S. states, the rape of a man was not reported as an incident of rape but as an assault. In many countries, the laws on human trafficking do not recognize men as victims; therefore, cases of men trafficked as laborers are not considered cases of human trafficking. In addition, many of the help service s offered to victims of trafficking (including those services offered in the United States) are female or child focused. Physically, victims of trafficking are often in poor health—after all they are perceived by their employers as essentially disposable—and because of their fear of the authorities, enforced by their employers' reports of government corruption, victims will resist aid from government officials in terms of social assistance and health care.

According to a 2006 report from Human Rights Watch (HRW), victims of labor trafficking, particularly those victims in domestic servitude, are abused in terms of health, safety, and medical care. According to HRW's report, domestic workers were often not provided a bedroom in the home in which they worked. Instead, these victims were expected to sleep in utility rooms or near gas furnaces, in unheated basements, or wherever they could find to rest. These domestic workers were also denied sufficient nutrition, forced to clean with vaporous cleaning products in closed areas, and expected to be on call at all hours of the day or night without a day off. The lack of health insurance and the restricted ability (or inability) to seek medical care if it was required were also reported by victims of labor trafficking. The HRW (2006) reports that workers were required to continue working even if they were ill.

> Victims of labor trafficking are forced to work against their will, by threats of harm to their families, and with their passports or identification cards in the possession of their employers.

> Victims of labor trafficking often do not realize that it is illegal for traffickers to dictate how they repay their debts.

It is also not unusual for victims of labor trafficking to suffer from malnutrition, poor personal hygiene, and untreated injuries such as lacerations or broken bones, or to have critical illnesses such as cancer or heart disease without the benefit of treatment. In fact, many of the trafficking victims of labor die while under their employment contracts. Despite these conditions, in most cases, the trafficked victims of labor will not volunteer information about their status or their abuse for fear of more abuse or deportation.

Most cases of labor trafficking have similar beginnings. One of the more common ploys for enticing someone into considering a move to the United States is the "maid scheme" (Richard, 1999). In maid schemes, it is suggested by the recruiter or trafficker that he or she is a part of the maid employment industry and that the recruiter's job is to locate maids and provide housekeeping services to customers, with commissions paid to the agency or service. Through an acquaintance from their country of origin (or an advertisement in the newspaper), the victim (often a female) will apply for the job and be transported to the United States by an "employee" of the agency. These women are usually between the ages of thirty-five and fifty-five, are looking for a way to support themselves and/or their family, and therefore enter the United States on a B-1 temporary visa (Richard, 1999). Once the victim arrives in the United States, the process is similar to that for a victim of sex trafficking in that the victims are taken to a "safe" house, their visas are confiscated by the traffickers, and they are expected to work long hours, with their salary paid directly to the "placement agency" of the traffickers. The victims remain in this arrangement through threats, intimidation, and/or physical abuse with little or no salary received from their traffickers.

Interestingly, victims of trafficking may relate to their traffickers in a manner similar to the hostages in Stockholm, Sweden, who established such a strong bond with their captors that many refused to testify against them on charges of kidnapping. Victims of trafficking, especially those victims isolated from everyone except fellow victims, sometimes form a relationship with their traffickers (as a defense mechanism and out of fear) and thus not want any harm to come to their traffickers. In some cases of labor trafficking, even when detected and ended by law enforcement officials, victims do not blame their traffickers for their victimization. Also, in some cases, human trafficking survivors will fail to see themselves as victims (Bales & Lize, 2007). In these cases, it is quite challenging for law enforcement officials to gain cooperation from illegal immigrants who have not complained about their abuse.

The same scenario applies to those victims of labor trafficking for domestic servitude; however, most often in these cases, the employer of the household seizes the visas of their victim. Once again, the victim does not seek help because of fear.

According to the U.S. Department of State (2004a), there are thousands of victims of labor trafficking in the United States every day. These victims are similar in background to the victims of sex trafficking as they are often brought to the United States from impoverished countries and expected to work under conditions that U.S. citizens will not tolerate. As more and more of the victims of labor trafficking are men, in addition to their work to support themselves, in many cases they also have to support their families both in the United States and outside of the United States. Therefore, the work of the trafficked laborer is perceived as necessary and his or her victimization is of minimal consequence.

Although it is most difficult to identify cases of labor trafficking, there are signs of labor trafficking victimization that are apparent to most. Specifically, the visible indicators of labor trafficking include (1) victims living within the same area in which they work or victims who are driven from home to work with an employed supervisor or the owner(s) of the establishment; (2) victims under the constant surveillance of their employer or other employees; and (3) victims whose translator will be either their employer or another employee when they want to communicate with someone outside of the workforce. Of course, as with any criminal action, signs or indicators of the activity do not prove the existence of the activity or indicate guilt; however, these signs should at least raise suspicion and warrant investigation.

> In 2006, a nightclub owner in Dallas was convicted of one count of forced labor and one count of conspiracy to commit forced labor. The owner imported young Korean women and forced them to work in his nightclub under conditions of fear and violence (Turkishpress.com, 2006).

For the employer, the labor of his or her trafficked victim continues as long as the abuse is not discovered. To further hide the abuse of laborers, employers will not seek medical treatment for their workers or will ask their acquaintances with some medical training to provide assistance to their victims. In addition, victims of labor trafficking are also moved by their employers from one area to another (especially those forced to work outside, without cover, in agriculture) and it is not unusual for an outsider to have contact with the trafficked individual only once or twice before he or she is moved and another trafficked victim is in his or her place.

> Many victims of labor trafficking develop Stockholm Syndrome, which is characterized by cognitive distortions of positive feelings developed by hostages for their captors. This bond may occur between the victims of labor trafficking and their traffickers (U.S. Department of Health and Human Services, 2005).

Finally, with Web sites in many diverse languages, the Internet becomes the preferred space targeted by business owners (Pehar, 2003) for locating people who can be trafficked. McCabe (2007) suggests that in more and more cases, the Internet is being used to support national and international criminal activity. In fact, more than 1,000 men in the United States each month make inquiries online to a mail-order bride business for not only wives but also domestic servants (Egan, 1996).

For individuals from other countries in need of employment and desiring a life in the United States, the opportunity to come to America in exchange for working as a nanny or a maid in an American home is wonderful. Even if the opportunities are for little more than a minimum wage job in a garment factory, the promise of a life in the United States is a wonderful dream. Therefore, there are always willing participants from countries outside of the United States who will approach labor traffickers for the opportunity of a better life for them and their families.

Offenders

In attempting to identify the perpetrators, offenders, or traffickers, one must acknowledge that, just as in the case of sex trafficking, labor traffickers are of all ages, sexes, races, and nationalities. Crucial to the discussions of these perpetrators is their method of obtaining their victims and the fact that most of the traffickers put up their own money as start-up costs for the trafficking (National Institute of Justice, 2004). Therefore, these initial contact individuals must give the appearance of a legitimate businessman who can provide opportunities for employment. Specifically, few (if any) individuals would sign up to be a slave; hence, traffickers must be very shrewd while attracting these individuals, and one of the most common methods for attracting victims is advertising. Individuals enter the United States with the hope of legitimate employment and a chance for a better life. Unfortunately, this better life is not always available. In a report on nine countries by Kangaspunta (2006), the number of suspects reported by the United Nations Office on Drugs and Crime (UNODC) was provided and the nationality of traffickers was examined. As shown in Table 3.1, in the majority of cases, traffickers were nationals of the country from which they trafficked people. However, common nationalities for at least two of the nine countries were Turkish, Bulgarian, Serb-Montenegrin, Ukrainian, and Romanian.

It is not unusual to discover male and female traffickers involved in the labor trafficking of men, women, and children. It is also not unusual to discover only female traffickers involved in the labor trafficking of women and young girls.

Table 3.1. Nationality of Labor Traffickers in Nine Countries

Country	Nationality of Traffickers				
Germany (n = 579)	German (56.1%)	Turkish (14.5%)	Bulgarian (11.7%)	Lithuanian (11.6%)	Polish (6.0%)
Greece (n = 261)	Greek (79.3%)	Albanian (8.4%)	Bulgarian (5.7%)	Egyptian (2.7%)	
Iceland (n = 4)	Chinese (100%)				
Montenegro (n = 21)	Serb-Montenegrin (85.7%)	Bosnian (9.5%)	Ukraine (4.8%)		
Netherlands (n = 118)	Dutch (51.7%)	Romanian (20.3%)	Bulgarian (17.8%)	Turkish (5.9%)	Nigerian (4.2%)
Portugal (n = 106)	Polish (53.8%)	Latvian (12.3%)	Estonian (12.3%)	Hungarian (11.3%)	Czech (10.3%)
Serbia (n = 35)	Serb-Montenegrin (88.6%)	Ukraine (5.7%)	Romanian (2.9%)	Bulgarian (2.9%)	
Slovenia (n = 13)	Slovenian (92.3%)	Bulgarian (7.7%)			
Switzerland (n = 5)	Italian (80.0%)	Swiss (20.0%)			

Note: Percentage rounded

Finally, one cannot dismiss the element of organized crime involved in labor trafficking. Traffickers have an added advantage in the trafficking women and girls from countries in which females are considered inferior to males (Richard, 1999): in these countries, criminal networks of traffickers take advantage of the abundance of cheap labor and will often recruit females for labor trafficking. In these cases, organized crime groups profit from both the trafficking fees and the labor of the victim(s). In fact, it is not unusual for criminal organizations involved in labor trafficking to use the trafficked person for other criminal purposes such as the transportation or selling of drugs.

In the United States, illegal aliens are smuggled into the country to harvest fruits and vegetables and to participate in other forms of manual labor only to owe thousands of dollars to their smugglers or field bosses (Lush, 2004). Field bosses traffic laborers through other bosses on the basis of the season of harvest. Perpetrators know that once they traffic their victims to the United States, threats against the victims' Green Card status, threats of deportation, and the victims' lack of knowledge of U.S. laws will keep the victims under their control (Crandall et al., 2005). Because of their ignorance of the laws and their distrust of law enforcement, victims of labor trafficking will deny their situations to government officials, thus, in effect, providing protection for their traffickers. The traffickers are aware that they have this protection from victim reports; hence, the activity continues in spite of U.S. laws against labor trafficking.

Selected expenses for illegal entry into the United States:

$10,000–$25,000 for fraudulent passports, $8,000 for bribes at bor-der checkpoints, and $4,000–$5,000 escort fees through transit points (National Institute of Justice, 2004).

U.S. Laws and Efforts

As the United States continues to be perceived as the land of opportunity, there continues to be the phenomenon of legal and illegal immigrants wish-ing to enter the country. Unfortunately, some of these individuals who have entered the country, and some of those individuals who have been born in the United States, are victims of labor trafficking. For those noncitizens of the United States, the laws governing entry into the country provide some pro-tection. Specifically, for those entering the United States (legally) for work, a visa or work permit is required. For those immigrants entering under a G-5 or A-3 visa, or the S visa, there are governmental limitations to regulate the balance between work and rest. Unfortunately, there is still little or no resolu-tion on the B-1 (temporary) visa. Once immigrants are within the country, the Immigration and Nationality Act (INA) provides rules for employment in the United States. Under the INA, employers are allowed to hire only legally recognized workers, with employers required to verify all employment documentation. The Fair Labor Standards Act (FLSA) established standards for minimum wage and overtime pay, and the Migrant and Seasonal Agricul-tural Worker Protection Act (MSPA) provides safety guidelines for work in migrant and seasonal agricultural work. However, in labor trafficking these laws are not obeyed. Specifically, as most victims of labor trafficking begin work without employment documentation or false documentation, there exists no record of their employment for review by the Department of Labor. In 1998, the attorney general announced the establishment of an interagency

Workers' Exploitation Task Force (WETF). The mission of the WETF is to investigate, prosecute, and prevent labor exploitation cases throughout the United States.

After passage of the Trafficking Victims Protection Act (TVPA), the FBI began to work with the Human Smuggling and Trafficking Center to assist in the detection and prevention of sex and labor trafficking within the United States.

Finally, with the use of the T visa, immigrants who have suffered abuse while in the United States at the hands of labor or sex traffickers will be offered the opportunity to stay in the United States with their family members (Richard, 1999). The T visa program, similar to the U visa program (for certain crime victims who have been hurt and are working with law enforcement officials) and the S visa program (for certain people helping in criminal investigations), is designed for victims of certain types of trafficking. The T visa is valid for up to three years and, with the T visa, there exists the possibility of applying for permanent residency in the United States.

In addition to laws aimed specifically at labor in the United States, the United States also spent more than $81 million on anti-trafficking efforts in fiscal year 2004 (U.S. Department of State, 2005). Of this money, approximately $30 million was spent on efforts to stop labor trafficking, including on programs in source countries of human trafficking for labor. Without documentation of their existence, there are no expectations of fair compensation or safety for the victims. Without funding to support governmental and nongovernmental efforts to end labor trafficking, there is no expectation of escape for the victims. Historically, in the U.S. labor system of monitoring or review, the victim of trafficking for labor is nonexistent. Today that is changing.

Summary

Labor trafficking involves the recruitment, harboring, transportation, provision, or obtaining of a person for labor or services, through the use of force, fraud, or coercion. Labor trafficking includes both bonded labor and forced labor, neither of which is a new crime in the United States.

Labor trafficking is more difficult to detect than is sex trafficking. The victims of labor trafficking are often hidden in plain sight and may be victimized for years before authorities are ever alerted. It is not unusual for victims of labor trafficking to suffer from malnutrition, poor personal hygiene, untreated injuries, and illnesses without medical care as perpetrators isolate their victims and, in many cases, confine them to their workplace.

Perpetrators of labor trafficking can be male or female, white or non-white, of all ages and nationalities. One of the most common methods used by perpetrators to attract victims is advertising for employment in agriculture, industry, or as a domestic servant such as a nanny. Individuals enter the United States with the hope of legitimate employment and a chance for a better life. Unfortunately, and on the contrary, these individuals become victims of labor trafficking who are abused and at times may even die. At the same time, the traffickers become richer through the forced labor of others.

Historically, governmental efforts to end abuse in the workplace have been limited to legal immigrants and workplace violence (McCabe & Martin, 2005). However, with the latest influx of illegal aliens into the country, the U.S. government is now beginning to address the problems and vulnerabilities associated with labor trafficking. Laws and funding related to labor trafficking are now established and more will come as we begin to identify more cases of labor trafficking, provide more services for the victims of labor trafficking, and prosecute more of those involved in human trafficking for labor.

Questions on Chapter 3

1. What is the difference between bonded and forced labor and why are these categories important to distinguish in discussions of labor trafficking?
2. Why has labor trafficking received even less attention than sex trafficking in the national and international arena?
3. What are three indicators of labor trafficking?
4. How do perpetrators of labor trafficking attract and obtain victims?
5. Once an individual is a victim of labor trafficking, his or her physical health often deteriorates. Why?

Questions for Further Thought

1. If individuals choose to indenture themselves, why would law enforcement or the U.S. public be concerned about the conditions of their labor?

2. Why would individuals from countries outside of the United States want to work in the United States?
3. Why does human trafficking for labor receive significantly less publicity than human trafficking for sexual exploitation?
4. If you were a U.S. business owner, would the possibility of trafficked labor appeal to you?
5. If trafficked victims are paid more than they would earn employed in similar work in their own country, is labor trafficking really such a problem?

· 4 ·

ENTERING THE UNITED STATES
AND U.S. RESPONSES

Thousands of individuals enter the United States legally each year. Those individuals contribute to the workforce, the tax base, and the culture of America. The U.S. government now recognizes that thousands of individuals also enter the United States illegally through smuggling or trafficking with either no documentation or false documentation. The victims of trafficking are the focus of this chapter. In 2004, the U.S. Department of State estimated that between 14,500 and 17,500 individuals are trafficked into this country annually. Of these individuals, some are trafficked against their will and some are trafficked under false pretenses. Regardless, cases of human trafficking have been reported in approximately one-half of the fifty states.

These trafficked individuals enter the United States on foot, come in vehicles that cross the Mexican or Canadian border, fly into the United States through international airports (on flights that often originate in the United Kingdom or other transit points outside of Asia), or enter the United States on fishing trawlers or freighters that enter U.S. harbors (Zhang & Chin, 2004; NCIS, 2005). Once these trafficked individuals have successfully crossed U.S. borders, they blend into the melting pot of America and are virtually unrecognizable. In fact, unless identified by an employer or another person living in the United States, these individuals may remain in the United States for their lifetime—a lifetime that could include neglect, abuse, coercion, and death at the hands of their traffickers.

> Unless victims of human trafficking are identified to law enforcement officers, once they cross U.S. borders, they blend into the melting pot of America.

The United States, with its label as "a land of milk and honey," is one of the most attractive countries for immigrants and has been since its foundation. Researchers such as Tiefenbrun (2002) suggest, in terms of trafficking victims, that the United States is one of the primary destinations for trafficked women, especially those women from the former Soviet Union, to work in the areas of prostitution and pornography. With the collapse of the Berlin Wall and the lack of physical barriers in Europe, movement between Eastern and Western Europe has become relatively easy, and with false U.S. entry documentation available for a fee, the move of a non-American into the United States may be a simple trip.

Recently, U.S. government officials have accused fourteen nations of failing to stop this modern-day slave trade, including Saudi Arabia and Kuwait, where trafficking victims have been identified on numerous occasions with little or no response from the foreign governments (News and Advance, 2005). Given that more than thirty-five countries have been identified as having individuals in forced labor in at least ninety different cities across the United States (Free the Slaves, 2006), the United States is now perceived as not only a prime destination but also a leader in the recognition of the magnitude of the problem. This recognition stems primarily from legislation. The U.S. legislation discussed in this chapter focuses on laws governing official entry into the country and laws to combat trafficking.

Entering the United States

Citizens of foreign countries who wish to enter the United States are required to have a visa, which is presented to immigration officials at U.S. borders for entry into the country. Visas are essentially classified according to the intention of the visitor: permanent (immigrant) and temporary (nonimmigrant).

Immigrant visas are for people who intend to live permanently in the United States (even if they are not planning to be employed in the United States). Three categories of immigrant visas are family, employment, and diversity program. In both family and employment-based visas, the immigrant must have a sponsor (either a relative or an employer). For the diversity visa, a lottery designed around a certain number of immigrants per country is used and an immigrant is selected through the lottery. The lottery visa does not require a sponsor; however, there are generally only a few openings available per country. The Department of Homeland Security (DHS) requires that they be notified of all immigrant visa applications.

The temporary or nonimmigrant visa categories essentially allow employment or training in the United States for a limited period. For each of the following nonimmigrant visa categories, approval from the DHS and U.S. Citizenship and Immigration Services (USCIS) is required:

F visa for students
H visa for temporary workers
J visa for specialists such as teachers or medical doctors
K visa for fiancé(e)s
L visa for employees in intracompany transfers
O visa for workers with extraordinary abilities
P visa for athletes and entertainers
Q visa for international cultural exchange visitors

The following nonimmigrant visas do not require approval from the DHS and USCIS:

E visa for treaty traders and investors
R visa for religious workers
TN visa for Canadian and Mexican professionals

In addition, individuals may enter the United States for business or tourism. Persons entering the United States on a visitor visa (B-1) or for tourism (B-2) are not allowed to work in the United States. Neither of these most commonly used visas requires the notification of the DHS or USCIS. Finally, visitors who are citizens of certain countries, such as Canada and Bermuda and who are visiting the United States for ninety days or less are not required to have a visa.

A visa does not guarantee entry into the United States as the DHS or USCIS may still deny admission to the United States. However, in most cases (especially before 9/11) the presentation of one's visa meant entry into the

United States. Since 9/11, all male nonimmigrant tourists and business applicants (B-2 and B-1) between the ages of sixteen and forty-five must complete a supplemental application form, as is the case with all student and exchange visitors. In addition, in October 2001, in reaction to 9/11, President George W. Bush established the DHS, with one of its goals being to monitor immigrant passage into the country and with an operating budget of approximately $90 million (Bodenheimer, 2003). In 2003, two new bureaus were established: the Bureau of Customs (BOC) and Immigration and Customs Enforcement (ICE). Both bureaus are responsible for monitoring entry into the United States and enforcement of immigration laws (Sundberg, 2004). However, in cases of human trafficking (and even terrorism), the monitoring of U.S. borders is not always the solution. As with any system, the limitation and vulnerability of the visa system are known to traffickers (Sundberg & Winterdyk, 2006).

It is suggested that the three most vulnerable areas in terms of documentation to enter the United States are related to the illegal use of visas, U.S. passports, and the Visa Waiver Program (VWP) (Richard, 1999). First, in the case of all visas, the duration of its validity may be related to its abuse. Specifically, the longer the multiple entry visa's duration, the more opportunity for its illegal use. In countries such as Mexico, Thailand, and the Philippines (all major source countries for human trafficking victims), visas may be valid for up to ten years. Business (B-1) and tourist (B-2) visas essentially go unchecked and are the easiest to obtain; hence, they are often easy to forge and use in cases of human trafficking. Finally, student (F1) visas, fiancé(e) (K1), and entertainer (P1 and P3) visas are also relatively easy to obtain, to falsify, and to acquire by traffickers (Richard, 1999).

Second, it is not unusual for Anglo-background individuals, particularly males, to be used as "jockeys" to escort victims of human trafficking into the country using a U.S. passport. In these cases, the individual will marry the woman (on paper) and escort her into the United States posing as her husband (or boyfriend) to answer the questions asked by immigration officials (Richard, 1999). These individuals escort the victims into the United States on an overnight or a holiday flight, when the number of immigration staff is lower, to avoid detection.

Finally, traffickers will often transit through Canada en route to the United States. As Canada participates in the U.S. VWP, and as Canada offers a VWP for Korean citizens, Korean victims are waived into Canada, then (after receiving false Canadian documents of citizenship) waived into the United States from Canada (Richard, 1999).

The major airports of entry are Los Angeles' LAX, New York's JFK, Miami International, and San Francisco International (Richard, 1999). In addition, Atlanta (with its multitude of nationalities and cited security breaches) has been identified as an emerging hub for human trafficking. In reaction, one of the country's earliest law enforcement units focused on the detection of human trafficking cases was established in Atlanta.

In summary, to enter the United States, visas are often confirmed through a reference to U.S. National Security. There are two major types of visas: an immigrant visa and a nonimmigrant visa. Immigrant visas are for those individuals who intend to live and work permanently in the United States. Nonimmigrant visas are for those individuals who wish to enter the United States temporarily for a specific purpose such as tourism, education, temporary work, or as a diplomat. Owing to the implied lack of permanency, the nonimmigrant visa is easier to obtain and is an area of vulnerability; it is more common to find victims of human trafficking with legal and illegal nonimmigrant visas.

> To enter the United States, a visa is required. There are two major types of visas: an immigrant visa and a nonimmigrant visa. Immigrant visas are for those individuals who intend to live and work permanently in the United States. Nonimmigrant visas are for those individuals who wish to enter the United States temporarily.

Nationals of qualified countries under the Visa Waiver Pilot Program (VWPP) are not required to have a visa if they are staying in the United States for less than ninety days. For example, Canadian citizens do not require a visa for a short trip to the United States. This is another vulnerable area for human trafficking, as some victims may appear to be Canadian nationals with false documentation of citizenship and enter the United States through Canada without a visa. Some of the vulnerabilities of the U.S. process of allowing entry into the country have been identified and legislative solutions have been sought to reduce the incidence of human trafficking.

Trafficking Laws

In 2000, the U.S. Congress and President Bill Clinton responded to the crisis of human trafficking by passing the Trafficking Victims Protection Act

(TVPA). This law not only identified the action of human trafficking but also provided stiffer prison penalties (ten to twenty years per count) for those convicted of human trafficking and life sentences to traffickers if a victim of human trafficking was killed. The TVPA provided a very broad definition of human trafficking to include those cases in which only psychological coercion (not physical) is used and those cases involving fraud in the representation of employment for the victims. The TVPA also laid out the framework for the creation of the Office to Monitor and Combat Trafficking in Persons under the U.S. Department of State, located in Washington, DC. The Office to Monitor and Combat Trafficking in Persons provides the most recent information on cases worldwide and also submits to Congress on an annual basis the *Trafficking in Persons* (*TIP*) report, which includes information on countries' efforts to eliminate severe forms of trafficking. This *TIP* analysis is based upon the prosecution, protection, and prevention efforts of countries as well as the rescue, removal, and reintegration efforts that focus on victims of human trafficking. This Act began the categorizing of countries in a tier system relating to their efforts to combat trafficking. It also provided a clearinghouse for information on trafficking victims worldwide.

Despite criticism that the Act contained inconsistencies in definition and in some practices weakened the protection for trafficked victims (Free the Slaves, 2006), the 2000 Act was critical in its recognition of the trafficked person as a victim, its distinction between human smuggling and human trafficking, its categorization of a country with "significant" victims as a country with a hundred plus victims of human trafficking, and its placement of countries into a tier system on the basis of historical and current efforts toward ending human trafficking. After 9/11, U.S. officials began to recognize the importance of international cooperation, and the *TIP* report is one example of this recognition (Sundberg & Winterdyk, 2006).

True to the U.S. criminal justice model of prevention, prosecution, and protection, the Act of 2000 laid out the framework for all U.S. efforts against human trafficking (Goodey, 2003). Today, the three minimum standards for the TVPA are that (1) the governments of countries should prohibit severe forms of trafficking in persons and should punish such acts and the persons responsible; (2) the governments of countries should prescribe punishment for sex trafficking involving force similar to that of forcible sexual assault; and (3) the governments should punish any act of a severe form of trafficking. For clarity, severe forms of trafficking include the sex trafficking of children (those under the age of eighteen) and the use of fraud or coercion for the purpose of involuntary servitude, debt bondage, or slavery. The fourth standard, later amended, states that governments should make serious and sustained efforts to eliminate human trafficking of all categories.

In 2003, the TVPA was further strengthened with the Trafficking Victims Protection Reauthorization Act (TVPRA) signed by President George W. Bush. The Act was again recognized by President Bush in 2005. The TVPRA not only addressed the limited resources of victims and the restrictions placed on them by the immigration authorities but also contained significant mandates for Departments of State, Labor, Homeland Security, and Health and Human Services and the U.S. Agency for International Development (U.S. Department of State, 2004). The fourth minimum standard, as revised in the TVPRA, calls for the use of ten criteria to assess whether a country is making serious and sustained efforts to eliminate trafficking. The TVPRA also created a "special watch list" of countries that should receive focused attention during the following year. This special watch list was established for countries in the Tier 2 classification that showed a significant number of victims in the severe form of trafficking category, a significant increase in the number of victims, or evidence that the country was failing to increase its efforts to end human trafficking (Krause, 2006). For the classification of countries into the various tiers, information is collected from U.S. embassies, consultants around the world, foreign ambassadors in Washington, and nongovernmental and international organizations working on human rights issues. Each year, as more and more countries have begun to recognize human trafficking, the list of countries in the tier system has increased. For example, in 2002, there were 89 countries ranked, and in 2003, there were 116.

> To further focus national efforts on ending human trafficking, countries are placed in categories (tiers) on the basis of their previous and current efforts to reduce human trafficking.

Also in 2003, the PROTECT Act was enacted to increase penalties for those who abuse children. Specifically, the Act strengthens law enforcement agencies' ability to prevent, investigate, prosecute, and punish those committing violent crimes against children. It also targets participants in sex tourism, as it includes a provision that Americans who sexually abuse children while abroad can face a prison term of up to thirty years (Miller, 2006). The Act has the authority to increase prison terms to up to twenty years for nonfamily abductions, provides two strikes legislation for those convicted twice of the serious sexual abuse of a child, and strengthens the prohibition of "virtual" child pornography. Finally, the PROTECT Act eliminates the statute of limitation, which expired at the child victim's age of twenty-five, on the abduction or physical or sexual abuse of children.

In 2004, the Federal Bureau of Investigation (FBI) began to work with the Human Smuggling Trafficking Center, which brings together federal agencies such as the DHS and the Central Intelligence Agency (CIA) to discuss cases of human trafficking and plans to end human trafficking. In 2004, the FBI also launched the National Hispanic Sex Trafficking Initiative to stop the sex trafficking of women into the United States from Mexico, Central America, and South America.

By focusing state and federal law enforcement efforts on the criminal activity of human trafficking, the message is sent to those involved in trafficking and the general public that the U.S. government is serious about its commitment to combating this problem; however, one cannot discount the importance of cooperative efforts among the various agencies if human trafficking is to end within the United States. Local and state law enforcement officials may have training in interviewing but may not have the history of investigating cases of human trafficking or the language proficiency required to speak to the victims. The federal officers within the Department of ICE, for example, are trained to investigate immigrant status and deportation procedures; although they may know the language of the victims, they may not have the training required for victim interviewing. Thus, these agencies must work together to secure corroborating testimony from trafficking victims and any possible witnesses (Bales & Lize, 2007). Provided investigators can gather the evidence, obtain witness testimony, and provide statements from the victims, trafficking cases are certainly prosecutable. However, investigating a case of human trafficking, given international borders, constant movement of victims, narrowly focused lines of communications between traffickers, and language and cultural barriers, is extremely difficult.

Tier Placement

The U.S. State Department and the Office to Monitor and Combat Trafficking in Persons (2005) have identified various tiers into which countries may be classified in terms of their efforts to comply with the TVPA and TVPRA. This identification determines whether a country is a country of origin, transit, or destination for a significant number of victims of severe forms of human trafficking. For clarity, a significant number indicates that the country has identified one hundred or more victims. The United States has been identified as a major country of destination, and countries that do not provide information on their number of human trafficking victims (such as Iraq) are not included in the tier placement. For an empirical assessment of the countries, see Appendix A. A specific narrative on Mexico can be found in Appendix B.

Tier 1 countries are defined as countries whose governments fully comply with the Act's minimum standards. Tier 2 countries are defined as countries that do not fully comply with the Act's minimum standards but are making significant efforts to bring themselves into compliance with those standards. Tier 3 countries are countries that do not fully comply with the minimum standards and are not making significant efforts to do so. For a comparison of the demographic characteristics of Tier 1 and Tier 3 countries, see Appendix C. The TVPRA added another category, the Tier 2 Watch List, which identifies countries placed in the second tier where (1) the absolute number of victims of severe forms of trafficking is very significant or is significantly increasing; or (2) there is a failure to provide evidence of increasing efforts to combat severe forms of trafficking in persons from the previous year; or (3) the determination that the country is making significant efforts to bring itself into compliance with minimum standards was based on commitments by the country to take additional steps over the next year. This identification of a country as being in the Tier 2 Watch List suggests that special efforts (U.S. and international) will be focused better preparing the country to end or reduce human trafficking. See Appendix D for a comparison of Tier 2 countries and Tier 2 Watch List countries.

Tier 1

There are twenty-five countries in Tier 1 identified in the 2004 *Trafficking in Persons* report: Australia, Austria, Belgium, Canada, Colombia, Czech Republic, Denmark, France, Germany, Ghana, Hong Kong, Italy, Republic of Korea, Lithuania, Macedonia, Morocco, The Netherlands, New Zealand, Norway, Poland, Portugal, Spain, Sweden, Taiwan, and the United Kingdom.

To further explain the measures taken by countries classified as Tier 1, the United Kingdom is used as an example. The United Kingdom fully complies with the minimum standards of the U.S. State Department and demonstrates strong efforts in law enforcement, prosecution, prevention, and victim protection. In 2005 and 2006, the United Kingdom conducted more than 500 trafficking investigations and prosecuted and convicted more than one dozen cases of trafficking for sexual exploitation and forced labor. Prison sentences in these cases ranged from five to more than twenty years for those convicted traffickers. In 2005, the United Kingdom passed the Serious Organized Crime and Police Act, which created a national law enforcement division to dismantle organized crime and human trafficking. In addition, the United Kingdom provides shelters in London for adult women who are victims of trafficking, and law enforcement continues to monitor Heathrow and Gatwick airports to identify at-risk and/or unaccompanied children.

Finally, the United Kingdom is probably one of the best countries (outside of the United States) in terms of addressing the phenomenon of child trafficking. Specifically, the nongovernmental organization End Child Prostitution and Trafficking (ECPAT) United Kingdom has provided venues for government and nongovernmental agencies to meet and discuss cooperative efforts to ending child victimization and has produced numerous reports, such as the 2004 *Cause for Concern? London Social Services and Child Trafficking*. In this report, Somerset (2004) details the U.K. perspective on child trafficking, provides information on London's resources in terms of social services for these victims, and provides guidance and recommendations for members of social services and other individuals wishing to assist these child victims. Finally, included in Somerset's report are examples to assist government officials in identifying some of the characteristics of child trafficking cases.

Tier 2

There are fifty-four countries in Tier 2 identified in the 2004 *Trafficking in Persons* report: Afghanistan, Albania, Angola, Argentina, Armenia, Bahrain, Belarus, Benin, Bosnia, Brazil, Bulgaria, Burkina Faso, Burundi, Cambodia, Cameroon, Chile, China, Costa Rica, Egypt, El Salvador, Finland, The Gambia, Guinea, Hungary, Indonesia, Iran, Israel, Kuwait, Kyrgyz Republic, Latvia, Lebanon, Malaysia, Mali, Mauritius, Moldova, Mozambique, Nepal, Nicaragua, Niger, Panama, Romania, Rwanda, Saudi Arabia, Singapore, Slovak Republic, Slovenia, South Africa, Sri Lanka, Switzerland, Togo, United Arab Emirates, Uganda, Ukraine, and Uzbekistan. One common characteristics of these countries is the support (although sometimes minimal) from their governmental organizations to reduce and/or end human trafficking within the country.

In 2006, China and Malaysia were placed on the Tier 2 Watch List as their governments had failed to show evidence of increasing efforts to address transnational trafficking (Krause, 2006).

Tier 2 Watch List

There are forty-three countries on Tier 2 Watch List identified in the 2004 *Trafficking in Persons* report: Azerbaijan, Belize, Bolivia, Democratic Republic of Congo, Côte d'Ivoire, Croatia, Cyprus, Dominican Republic, Estonia, Ethiopia, Gabon, Georgia, Greece, Guatemala, Honduras, India, Jamaica, Japan, Kazakhstan, Kenya, Laos, Madagascar, Malawi, Mauritania, Mexico, Nigeria, Pakistan, Paraguay, Peru, Philippines, Qatar, Russia, Senegal, Serbia-Montenegro, Suriname, Tajikistan, Tanzania, Thailand, Turkey, Vietnam, Zambia, and Zimbabwe. Many of these countries are in transition from less developed to developed economies, from high mortality rates to lower mortality rates, and from high rates of poverty to lower rates of poverty.

Explanations of the Tier 2 and Tier 2 Watch List classifications of countries can be given using Afghanistan, Nicaragua, and Zambia as examples. Afghanistan is a source country for women and children. Included in the efforts of the country to end human trafficking are projects such as the Transitional Islamic State of Afghanistan's establishment of a Child Trafficking Commission, workshops on child trafficking conducted by UNICEF, and meetings held by the Ministry of Hajj and Religious Affairs for Islamic clergy to discuss human trafficking and rally their support for efforts to end the criminal activity.

Nicaragua is also in the Tier 2 and is a source country for the trafficking of children. In addition, Nicaragua has been identified as a transit country for victims being moved from their countries to other destination countries. In 2003, its government designed and implemented a countrywide effort to end child trafficking. Although Nicaragua lacks effective law enforcement strategies, prosecutors have successfully convicted several individuals for severe human trafficking and utilize the resources of NGOs in their attempt to identify the perpetrators and victims of child trafficking.

Zambia has also been recognized as a source and transit country for women and children as child prostitution and trafficking exists in most of the urban centers. In addition, Zambia is one of the more central transit points for regional trafficking to South Africa. In 2003, the Ministries of Labor and Information and Broadcasting began public campaigns to raise awareness of child labor laws. In addition, NGOs have registered and returned approximately one hundred victimized children to their home villages.

> The TVPRA added the Tier 2 Watch List category on the basis of a country's number of victims of human trafficking and its efforts to reduce the number of cases of human trafficking.

Tier 3

There are ten countries in Tier 3 identified in the 2004 *Trafficking in Persons* report: Bangladesh, Burma, Cuba, Ecuador, Equatorial Guinea, Guyana, North Korea, Sierra Leone, Sudan, and Venezuela. There are fourteen countries in Tier 3 identified in the 2005 *Trafficking in Persons* report: Bolivia, Burma, Cambodia, Cuba, Ecuador, Jamaica, Kuwait, North Korea, Qatar, Saudi Arabia, Sudan, Togo, United Arab Emirates, and Venezuela. The classification of countries may change each year according to their performance in combating human trafficking, as evaluated by the Office to Monitor and Combat Trafficking in Persons. For example, in one year, Bolivia, Jamaica, Kuwait, Saudi Arabia, Togo, and the United Arab Emirates dropped from Tier 2 to Tier 3, and Cambodia and Qatar dropped from Tier 2 Watch List to Tier 3. During the same period (2004–2005), Bangladesh, Equatorial Guinea, Ghana, and Sierra Leone moved from Tier 3 to Tier 2 or Tier 2 Watch List classifications.

Bangladesh is a source and transit country for men, women, and children for the purposes of sexual exploitation, involuntary domestic service, child camel jockeying, and debt bondage for the fishing industry. It is also a source country for child trafficking for commercial sexual exploitation, bonded labor, and other forms of forced labor. It is one of the poorest countries in the world. Women and children from Bangladesh are sex trafficked to India and Pakistan and labor trafficked to the Gulf regions. In some cases, a trafficker living outside of the country will enter the country, marry a woman, and then sell her into bonded labor or prostitution.

Bangladeshi men are trafficked to Malaysia and Jordan for work in either construction or the garment industry. Bangladesh is also often used as a transit country for those trafficked from Burma en route to India. One of the major problems in Bangladesh is child trafficking, which is compounded by the country's low rate of birth registration. Since children with no legal birth documents are unable to prove citizenship or age, they are targets for traffickers. This is especially the case with young girls trafficked to India for sex and for young boys trafficked to the United Arab Emirates to work as camel jockeys. Border patrols and police efforts in addressing human trafficking are limited or nonexistent in Bangladesh, and traffickers are aware of this fact. Nongovernmental organizations have identified more than twenty vulnerable areas for human trafficking along the country's borders. Children from Bangladesh are also trafficked for organs, as the younger the child, the more likely the organs are healthy and HIV negative.

Burma is a source country for men and women trafficked for forced labor and sexual exploitation. Burmese women and children are trafficked to countries such as Thailand, China, Malaysia, and South Korea, where they are forced into commercial sexual exploitation, domestic servitude, or forced labor. Burmese children are trafficked to Thailand to work as street hawkers and beggars. Within the country, children are trafficked for sex and labor and to work as child soldiers. The military's use of forced labor is one of the main causes of child trafficking in the country. In addition to the trafficking of women for sex and labor and the trafficking of children for use as soldiers within the country, men and boys from the poor agricultural regions are trafficked from Burma to other countries such as China and India for sexual exploitation and forced labor. The criminal organizations for human trafficking within the country appear to be small scale and primarily freelance; however, most of their activity continues without acknowledgment by law enforcement. The government of Burma has made little effort to limit human trafficking and restricts the information released on human trafficking; therefore, the prevalence of human trafficking is unknown.

Cuba is a source country for women and children trafficked for sexual exploitation and forced child labor and has been identified as a destination for sex tourism. Cuban adults and children are also trafficked for forced labor in commercial agriculture, such as tobacco farming. There are also reported cases of Cubans being trafficked to the United States for debt bondage. Cuba's thriving sex trade caters to thousands of tourists every year from Europe, Latin America, and North America and involves not only the young boys and girls who are victims of abuse but also the state-run hotel workers, cab drivers, and police officers who may identify the commercial sex areas for those interested in participating in sexual exploitation. There appears to be little in terms of governmental help or nongovernmental organization initiatives to end human trafficking, especially sex trafficking, in Cuba. Again, because of the closed nature of the government, the prevalence of human trafficking is unknown.

Ecuador is a source, transit, and destination country for human trafficking. A major destination for Ecuadorian victims is Western Europe, and, in particular, Italy and Spain. Children are also trafficked from the coastal and border regions of Ecuador to the urban areas of the country for sexual exploitation or to work as forced labor on banana plantations. Much of the child trafficking occurs because poverty-stricken parents sell their children to traffickers, with or without knowledge of their abused futures. In addition, Colombian women and children are sex trafficked into Ecuador. Although little information exists on the amount of human trafficking within Ecuador on an annual basis, and government officials are only beginning to provide information on child trafficking, it is acknowledged by governmental and nongovernmental organizations that most of the internal trafficking of children within the country occurs for prostitution.

Equatorial Guinea is a transit and destination country for women and children trafficked for forced labor, domestic servitude, and commercial sexual exploitation. Children from Equatorial Guinea are trafficked from surrounding countries to work in the agricultural and commercial sectors of the country. These countries include Benin, Cameroon, and Nigeria for forced domestic and farm labor, and Malabo for forced commercial labor in the oil fields. Equatorial Guinea is also a destination country for human trafficking, with women and girls in prostitution in the country from Benin and Cameroon. In addition to adult trafficking, children from Guinea are trafficked to Western and Central Africa for forced sexual exploitation, domestic servitude, and/or to work as street beggars. As Equatorial Guinea is a country in which children as young as six are regularly seen working, it is primarily a destination country for child trafficking as the trafficked children will often blend into the mainstream of child workers. Child traffickers are aware of the need for labor in the country and are willing to supply child victims. Major concerns of the U.S. government are this child trafficking into the country for labor and Equatorial Guinea's lack of labor laws to control child labor.

Guyana is a country of source, transit, and destination for young women and children trafficked mainly for sexual exploitation, with many of the reported cases involving internal trafficking. Male victims of human trafficking from Guyana often end up in forced labor conditions in timber camps. Most of the human trafficking within Guyana takes place in the remote mining camps. Those women and children from Guyana who are trafficked out of the country are destined for countries such as Barbados, Trinidad, and the United States. Those women and children trafficked into Guyana are trafficked from Brazil.

In terms of internal trafficking, there is little in the way of government oversight or law enforcement. In fact, the adults and children lured to the mining or timber camps go in search of employment as highly paid employees but are restrained through debt bondage and/or violence and forced to work as either laborers or prostitutes. One of the issues of greatest concern for the U.S. government is the increasing amount of child labor within the country and the increasing number of victims.

North Korea is a source country for human trafficking. North Korea has suffered a food shortage for nearly two decades, and more than two million North Koreans have starved to death. As a result, many adults and children from North Korea have attempted to leave the country. China is the most accessible country for North Koreans; however, their illegal status within the country creates an even more difficult situation in that they are often at the mercy of the traffickers for survival, and if a native is returned to the country after attempting to leave illegally, he or she is often punished through hard prison labor. North Korea has no known laws specifically addressing the problem of human trafficking, and therefore the criminal activity continues. Traffickers, often members of organized crime networks, know of the vulnerabilities of those poor individuals and often purchase young women and children from their families for "work" in China or in other countries. Of course, many of the victims of human trafficking are unable to speak Chinese or English and are held as prisoners for forced labor or prostitution. As there is essentially no information released from the government on human trafficking, there are no real estimates on the number of victims of trafficking. However, it is not uncommon for young girls to be sold as brides.

Sierra Leone is a source, transit, and destination country for women and children trafficked for forced labor and sexual exploitation. Within the country, individuals are trafficked for work in domestic servitude and the commercial sex industry or for forced agricultural labor. Women and children from Sierra Leone are trafficked to Nigeria, Liberia, and other West African countries for both sex and labor. Women from Liberia and Guinea are trafficked into Sierra Leone for work in mining camps and in prostitution. Finally, Sierra Leone serves as a transit country for those being trafficked to Lebanon, across Europe, and to North America. Sierra Leone is an extremely poor African nation with a high level of economic inequality. Therefore, there is always a market for domestic servitude and other forms of forced labor, and traffickers, often thought to be family members or friends of families, will lure victims from their homes with promises of education and/or employment. Again, the government of Sierra Leone does not give estimates of trafficking and provides little or no assistance to victims of human trafficking within the country.

Sudan is a source country for victims of human trafficking and it may also be a transit and destination country for Ethiopian women. The continuous civil wars within the Republic of Sudan have led to the displacement of approximately four million people from their homes. For a trafficker, this situation is a dream come true as both adults and children are actively seeking the opportunity to rebuild and prosper. Women and children are sex trafficked within the country and across the borders into countries such as Uganda and Congo. Children and women are also trafficked for sex and labor to the United Arab Emirates and Qatar. Of concern for the U.S. government is the fact that Sudan has not adopted legislation that successfully addresses slavery or the trafficking of children as young boys are often trafficked as camel jockeys or as cooks, porters, and warriors for terrorist rebel organizations such as the Lord's Resistance Army (LRA), and law enforcement essentially turns a blind eye to the problem.

Finally, Venezuela is source, transit, and destination country for women and children trafficked for sexual exploitation and forced labor. Destination countries include Spain, the Netherlands, Mexico, and Aruba, while women and children from countries such as Brazil, Colombia, and Ecuador are trafficked into Venezuela for commercial sexual exploitation and domestic servitude. It is suggested by the Venezuelan government that organized criminal groups, especially those from Colombia, facilitate human trafficking in the country as an accompaniment to the drug trafficking trade. As the Venezuelan government reports extremely high rates of domestic violence and child prostitution, law enforcement attention is not likely to be focused on human trafficking, even the trafficking of children. Historically, government officials have not acknowledged a problem with human trafficking in the country.

For countries classified in Tier 3, there are usually certain U.S. sanctions. For example, the government may withhold nonhumanitarian and non-trade-related assistance such as in cultural and educational exchange programs. In addition, countries in the Tier 3 classification will not be provided with U.S. assistance from financial institutions such as the World Bank. As stated, in 2005, the United States identified fourteen countries that could be subject to sanctions for their failure to reduce human trafficking. As the categorization occurs on an annual basis, no country is placed in a tier permanently. As efforts to reduce human trafficking in Tier 3 countries increase, the countries may move to other tier placements.

Iraq may be a source country for women and children trafficked for the purposes of labor and sexual exploitation. Iraq is not ranked in the tier system because of its current state of political transition.

Challenges

As with any criminal activity, human trafficking poses challenges for law enforcement and prosecution. The first and greatest challenge is related to the fact that many of the victims of human trafficking are in the United States illegally; thus, they are often treated in the same manner (deported) as other undocumented workers.

The United States is one of the most aggressive countries in its fight against human trafficking. As a result of the TVPRA, the Justice Department now provides grants to states, units of local government, Indian tribes, and nonprofit nongovernmental organizations to develop and strengthen services for trafficking victims (U.S. Department of Labor, 2002). Also, because of the human trafficking legislation, the T visa was established to allow victims of severe forms of human trafficking to become temporary residents of the United States. The T visa is a direct U.S. government response to research findings that suggest that because of violence or threats of violence, the home country of trafficking victims is often not the best place for them to live once the victimization is discovered. After three years, recipients of a T visa may be eligible for permanent residency in the United States if (1) they are of good moral character, (2) they have complied with any reasonable request for assistance in the investigation of their cases, and (3) they are likely to suffer further victimization if they are removed from the United States.

Another challenge faced in the United States in terms of ending human trafficking is the lack of resources dedicated to investigating marriage fraud. As spousal prostitution, the K visa, and mail-order brides remain essentially unregulated, those involved in human trafficking have recognized an opportunity for human trafficking. However, U.S. officials are beginning to recognize these areas of vulnerability and are working toward increasing efforts to end the cases of human trafficking existing under the umbrella of marriage and family.

Finally, the United States has recognized that simply allowing the victim of human trafficking to remain in the country is not sufficient. In many cases, when the operation of a human trafficking ring ends, so does the ability of the victims to work and survive. By providing food, shelter, and job training to victims of human trafficking, the U.S. government has begun to recognize the importance of helping these individuals.

In 2004, it was estimated that approximately 16,000 people were trafficked into the United States for either labor or sexual exploitation. According to the FBI, human trafficking generates more than $9 billion in annual revenue. To date the U.S. government has provided approximately $400 million to support global anti-trafficking efforts (Hindustantimes.com, 2006) and more than $18 million a year to monitor U.S. borders (Bodenheimer, 2003).

In addition to these efforts and financial resources, agencies such as the Office for Victims of Crime (OCV), the Office of Refugee Resettlement (ORR), and the National Domestic Violence Hotline are attempting to assist the U.S. victims of human trafficking. Whether it is an issue of human rights, a concern over social responsibility, or an issue of health, the United States has been an active participant (if not a leader) in the efforts around the globe to end human trafficking.

Summary

Each year thousands of individuals are trafficked into this country despite heightened security measures to identify those individuals not born in the United States. Some of those individuals are trafficked against their will and some are trafficked under false pretenses. Whether these individuals enter the United States on foot, or come in vehicles that cross the Mexican or Canadian border, or fly into the United States on international flights, once they have successfully crossed U.S. borders, they are blended into the melting pot of America and pass virtually unrecognized.

To enter the United States, those born outside of the country are required to have either an immigrant visa or a nonimmigrant visa. Nonimmigrant visas, because of the implied lack of permanency, are an area of vulnerability in terms of human trafficking. In 2000, 2003, and 2005, the United States supported legislation to address human trafficking. As a result, countries were categorized in a tier system related to their efforts to combat trafficking. These countries are identified as Tier 1 countries, whose governments fully comply with the Act's minimum standards; Tier 2 countries, which do not fully comply with the Act's minimum standards but are making significant efforts to bring themselves into compliance with those standards; and Tier 3 countries, which do not fully comply with the minimum standards and are not making significant efforts to do so. A fourth category is the Tier 2 Watch List.

To end human trafficking, U.S. efforts have focused on three areas: supply, demand, and the traffickers. On the supply side, conditions that foster human trafficking must be recognized. For those countries of origin, economic opportunities (other than illegal opportunities) and educational opportunities must be created.

On the demand side, persons who exploit trafficked persons (for either labor or sex) must be identified and punished. U.S. efforts have historically focused on legislative efforts; however, now the U.S. focus is on enforcement and punishing those who perpetuate the victimization of these individuals.

Finally, at the trafficker level, law enforcement has begun identifying traffickers and trafficking routes. Prosecutors have begun to seek harsher penalties against those convicted of human trafficking. Through clear definition and coordination of law enforcement responsibility, traffickers seeking to profit from the trade may find themselves rewarded not with profit but with arrest and prison terms.

Questions on Chapter 4

1. How do citizens from other countries enter the United States legally?
2. In terms of travel visas, which category is most vulnerable to human trafficking and why?
3. Why was the U.S. Office to Monitor and Combat Trafficking in Persons established?
4. What is the purpose of the tier system as related to U.S. efforts to reduce human trafficking?
5. What are the categories and criteria of the tier system? Why was the Tier 2 Watch List established?

Questions for Further Thought

1. Why is a clearinghouse important in the study of human trafficking?
2. Why should the U.S. government fund efforts and programs outside of U.S. boundaries to fight human trafficking?

3. Why has the United Kingdom also become a pioneer in the fight to end human trafficking?
4. Do you believe you could predict the prevalence of human trafficking cases by studying the demographics of a country?
5. What else can the United States do to eliminate human trafficking?

· 5 ·

CHILD TRAFFICKING

When discussing the trafficking of persons, much of today's research focuses on the trafficking of women, their stories, and the conditions in which adult trafficking has occurred. The Federal Bureau of Investigation (FBI) has estimated that human trafficking generates $9 billion annually (Morrissey, 2006). Unfortunately, human trafficking is not limited to adult victims: children, some of whom are very young, constitute approximately one-half of all trafficking victims (Miller, 2006).

Child trafficking is often identified in reports of human trafficking; however, specific information on young victims is limited with regard to the number of children trafficked, the conditions of child trafficking, and the perpetrators behind child trafficking. In 2003, the United Nations identified the trafficking of minors for sex and labor as a serious global issue and one worthy of not only public attention but also legislative attention (NCIS, 2005). Also in 2003, the Prosecutorial Remedies and Other Tools to end the Exploitation of Children Today (PROTECT) Act was adopted to seek and punish aggressively those Americans involved in traveling to participate in child sex rings (Miller, 2006). However, day after day in the United States, one case after another is discovered involving a trafficked child and his or her exploitation.

United States v. Satia and Nanji (2001)

Two Maryland defendants have been convicted of holding a fourteen-year-old Cameroonian girl prisoner and forcing her to work as a domestic servant in their home. They were each sentenced to 108 months in prison.

In the late 1980s, Campagne and Poffenberger (1988) suggested that there were approximately 150,000 victims of child prostitution in the United States; however, their estimates did not distinguish between national and international minors or child prostitutes who chose to sell their bodies and children who are forced into a life of sexual exploitation. Regardless of choice or force, in the United States it is illegal to have sex with a child (McCabe, 2003). Researchers estimate that approximately two million people are slaves in the international sex market and that many of these individuals are children (Zoba, 2003). UNICEF estimates that more than 200 million children between the ages of five and seventeen are forced to work in situations of child bondage. Bales (2000) suggests that there are more slaves today than were ever taken from Africa.

In the global arena, the United States has been a leader in attempting to support the rights of children and to end child abuse (McCabe, 2003). With AMBER alerts for missing children, and Megan's Law, it is difficult to believe that child trafficking might occur in the United States; however, it does, and at a cost in terms of both human and economic capital (Schauer & Wheaton, 2006). Of course, the trafficking of women in the United States is much more extensive than the trafficking of children; however, child trafficking appears to be a growing issue within this country (Richard, 1999).

Research on immigrants has traditionally been conceptualized around adult men's movements, with women and children typically accompanying these men as a family (King, 2002); however, with child trafficking, a new aspect of immigration and abuse emerges. Estes and Weiner (2001) suggest that nearly 10,000 children between the ages of ten and seventeen are brought into the United States from other countries annually for sex and that most of these children are forced to work in the sex industry. Reports from the National Center for Missing and Exploited Children suggest that in the 1980s the outlawed American motorcycle gangs were heavily involved in the trafficking of vulnerable youths and runways for prostitution and that those gangs moved their victims from one country to another; however, these gangs appear to have little involvement in child trafficking today.

The Youth Advocate Program International (2004) suggests not only that children are prostituted worldwide (and that the prostitution of girls as young as age five is prevalent) but also that children comprise a significant percentage of the slave labor force and in many cases are forced to work until they are physically unable to do so, and die. Mirkinson (1997) offers similar findings in reports of children (boys and girls as young as eight years old) for sale across the world for sex and/or labor. These are supported by the International Labour Organization's (ILO) identification of the 137 worst countries in terms of forced child labor, all of which are receiving U.S. trade benefits.

Finally, Estes and Weiner (2001) document that the trafficking of children is not only an international problem but also a U.S. concern, as some children who are U.S. citizens are now being trafficked within the country and to countries outside of the United States. Adults have a "shelf life"; they can be sold again and again until they have reached a certain age and are no longer marketable (Miller, 2006). Children are even more valuable. In today's age of focus on child abuse and child victimization, one can only ask, "How does this happen" or "Why does this happen?" The answers may be more rationally, economically based than many of us can imagine.

For clarity, the trafficking of children or those victims under the age of eighteen refers to the category of trafficking identified in the 2003 Trafficking Victims Protection Reauthorization Act (TVPRA) as a severe form of trafficking. However, as trafficked children are usually subsumed under the classification of women and children, little is known about the exact number of children trafficked in the United States and around the world annually. In addition, as it is often difficult to determine a child's age through physical characteristics alone, distinguishing between a child and a young man or woman is nearly impossible.

It is suggested by the U.S. government that approximately 50,000 women and children are trafficked into the United States annually and that the average age of those individuals (although older than the global average) is around twenty (Richard, 1999). Given the estimates of age, it is safe to conclude that many of those individuals are significantly under the age of twenty and, therefore, can be classified as children; however, as the overwhelming majority of known victims of human trafficking are involved in prostitution and sexual exploitation, and as the United States has historically not included male prostitutes within the definition of the crime of prostitution, these known adult and child victims are disproportionately female.

There is little empirical evidence to support the idea that a significant number of men are trafficked; however, a survey for law enforcement agencies in 2005 suggests that both male and female children are exploited through human trafficking (McCabe, 2007), and these findings are supported by researchers in the United Kingdom who suggest young men are victims of human trafficking for both forced labor and sexual exploitation (Somerset, 2004).

Researchers who attempt to generate a profile of child victims of human trafficking often use cases from source institutions and nongovernmental organizations for which age and gender are known (Kangaspunta, 2006). It is from these cases that it is determined that child victims comprise the largest percentage of the persons reported as victims of human trafficking outside the United States (although this is not the reality in the United States). It is also from these cases that it is concluded that most child victims come from families with many (four or more) children and with only one or two of the family members contributing to the family income (Kangaspunta, 2006). Hence, the trafficking of a child is profitable not only for the trafficker but also in many ways for the child's family. Specifically, even if family members are not paid for the children to be trafficked, they can save the economic cost of caring for the children. In addition, as stated in the case of adult trafficking, family members may allow children to travel with the trafficker to the United States or another country for the opportunity of work or a better life away from their native country.

Apart from their family background, which may also include domestic violence (McCabe, 2003), children who become victims of human trafficking may do so through their own ignorance of human trafficking and their desire to leave the family (Kangaspunta, 2006). In these cases, the children volunteer to be smuggled into a country only to discover later that they are now victims of child trafficking.

Child sex tourism involves people traveling from their country to another to engage in sex with a child. Recently prosecuted cases of child sex tourism have involved a U.S. pediatrician, a U.S. dentist, and a U.S. university professor (U.S. Department of State, 2005).

Why Children Are Trafficked

More than 1,000 Guatemalan babies are trafficked every year for adoption by couples in North America and Europe (UNICEF, 2006).

To understand the trafficking of children, one must first view the situation economically, with the child as the product and the purchaser as the consumer. The trafficker in this scenario is the businessperson who provides the product to the consumer. Children are trafficked for many reasons, including labor, adoption, drug smuggling, sex, for the supply of healthy internal organs, and (in some countries) soldiering and camel jockeying. Each use of a child means profit to his or her owner or trafficker. Currently, there is no national system for tracking unaccompanied minors; therefore, the movement of these children from place to place and from country to country is often accomplished without restriction.

Many foreign children enter the United States on a family immigration visa. With the family member visa, the child is sponsored by an individual within the United States (such as an uncle, aunt, cousin, or an individual claiming to be a relative) and allowed entry into the country. Children who appear to be at least eighteen years old also may enter the United States under false temporary (nonimmigrant) visas. Unless the child's documentation is determined to be false and the child is identified and taken into the custody of immigration officials on his or her attempt to enter the country, he or she is virtually undetectable (unless a random encounter occurs with law enforcement while within a country's borders) and therefore at the mercy of the trafficker.

As many as fourteen victims from the town of Chihuahua, Mexico, may have been kidnapped and their organs trafficked for transplants within the United States (Miles, 2003).

Empirical work in the area of forced labor indicates that many of the persons, including children, identified as working in exploitative conditions (including domestic servitude) gave their consent and, therefore, are of little interest to the criminal justice system (Munro, 2006). Again, as the lines between trafficking and smuggling are often blurred, the notion of consent (even for a child who cannot legally provide consent) leaves law enforcement officials conducting very few investigations in terms of labor exploitation.

Many children are placed in these positions of servitude by their parents or caregivers (Melrose, 2002). The majority of these children continue to work under deployable conditions without complaint and without attempting to leave their environment. In addition, many of these child victims do not report their abuse as they are often terrified to return home given that their parents or another family member essentially "sold" them into slavery (Melrose, 2002).

Attempts to determine whether any financial yield is received by the trafficked children suggest that for the most part the child victim receives little or no compensation; however, some researchers have suggested that with child forced labor, children often receive approximately 20% of the money they have earned (Mirkinson, 1997). For a child from a country mired in poverty, it is a wonderful opportunity to obtain some money (even if it is one-fifth of their earnings in the United States), and therefore the child accepts the abuse (which may include sexual abuse) as part of the working conditions. Government officials are now recognizing the involvement of organized crime in many cases of illegal adoptions through child trafficking. Specifically, in international cases revealed over the past few years, there have been a number of organized child trafficking rings involved in the criminal activity (Binh, 2006). These crime organizations provide infants to foreign couples (some from America) seeking to adopt. The traffickers involved in these types of organizations typically purchase babies from the poorest of families, orphanages, or single mothers. The babies are sold to the highest bidder.

As the children's health is a concern to their captor, they also receive food and shelter. This food and shelter, which for many far exceeds the conditions they left in their homeland, is an attractive incentive for the children and their parents, and hence the exploitation continues.

The process continues and children work in below-standard conditions in agriculture, mining, or manufacturing and for less than minimum wage to fulfill a bargain made by their parents for a better life for the children and their families. This arrangement works well for the traffickers; they receive money from the labor of the children, and in many cases the children are required to repay the trafficker the cost of their passage to the United States. Human trafficking is a profitable enterprise for all of the traffickers involved and for the parents of the children trafficked. Children provide an added benefit to their traffickers in that they are easier to control than adults, have a longer working-time potential, and, in many countries, are more in number and easier to obtain than adults are; thus, children for victimization through human trafficking are desired by traffickers.

In many ways children are easier targets for human trafficking than are adults. At entry into the United States, they often require less detailed identification information, and once they enter the United States they are easier to control.

As stated, illegal adoptions may be another reason for the trafficking of children. In particular, childless couples in the United States generate a demand for trafficked children (BBCNews.com, 2005). Specifically, as there always exists a demand in the United States and across Europe for white new-born babies (in particular boys), and with U.S. couples willing to pay $20,000 or more for a baby, a demand is always present. In the children's country of origin (including many of those countries previously governed by the Soviet Union), traffickers will identify possible children or babies on the basis of their physical characteristics and/or the physical characteristics of their parents and then either attempt to purchase the children from their parents or kidnap the children. No one was more surprised than the citizens of the United States when, in the 1990s, it was revealed that American companies such as the Gap and Nike were selling items made in sweatshops with forced and sometimes trafficked child labor (Bales, 2004). In cases such as these, the criminals were the "respectable" businesspeople and the product was something that everyone in the country desired. This realization that child trafficking affects American culture was a wake-up call for many in the United States.

In the United States, children born to unwed mothers (and especially children born to single white mothers or white drug-dependent mothers) are targeted and trafficked within the country for adoption. In a nutshell, individuals involved in the trafficking of babies understand this demand in the United States for children; often victims with the desired physical characteristic of "whiteness" are the targets of traffickers for illegal adoptions in the United States.

> Many childless U.S. couples have such a desire for a baby that the fact that the child may be a trafficking victim is not important (BBCNews. com, 2005).

Another reason for the trafficking of children is drug smuggling. According to Estes and Weiner (2001), children now serve as "drug mules" in transporting illegal narcotics from other countries into the United States. Historically, adult men and even women who appeared to be pregnant were used to transport drugs, particularly from Mexico and South America, into the United States; however, as security measures have increased and the searching of baggage and persons has become more prevalent in airports and land border crossings, individuals, including children, are transporting drugs by means of ingestion. Children often do not receive the scrutiny of U.S. customs or immigration officials as they enter the country as long as they are accompanied by an adult, and therefore children are excellent for use as drug mules. In the unfortunate event that the small plastic bag that is swallowed by the drug mule leaks into the stomach, death is a common outcome. However, as the trafficked child is viewed as cheap, disposable, and easy to replace, the perpetrator involved in drug smuggling actually loses less with a child than with an adult as the host if he or she dies while attempting to smuggle drugs.

United States v. Quinton Williams (2003)

A Nevada defendant has been convicted of sex trafficking a sixteen-year-old across the country by car through the states of Indiana, Texas, Arizona, and Nevada. He was sentenced to 125 months in prison.

The reason for the trafficking of children given most coverage by the media and most empirically investigated is sexual exploitation. Davidson (2005) identifies the children in the sex trade across the globe. McCabe (2007) focused on the children involved in trafficking for reasons of pornography, and Somerset (2004) discussed the children trafficked for prostitution. Among the reasons for the sex trafficking of children are child pornography, child prostitution, sex rings, molestation, the supporting sex tourism industry, and nude dancing (Campagne & Poffenberger, 1988; McCabe, 2003). As sex involving children is supported by the human desire for gratification, profit, and fulfillment, it is neither a phenomenon easily remedied nor an activity easily identified and/or investigated.

Many individuals, including recruiters, trainers, purveyors, creators of false documentation, transporters, money collectors, enforcers, and parents, are involved in the sex trafficking of children (Estes & Weiner, 2001). Sex involving a child sells, and traffickers are aware of the profits. Whether these children are born in the United States or brought into the country under the legalized family immigrant visa, through the unregulated industry of mail-order brides, or under false pretenses, all of these individuals are possible victims of child trafficking and all are trafficked for a profit.

The sex trafficking of children provides income for many involved in the enterprise, including in some instances organized criminal networks. Recent work by the United Nations Office of Drugs and Crime (UNODC) suggests the existence of a strong link between child sex trafficking and organized crime (Kangaspunta, 2006). This includes the payment of debts to criminal organizations through the exchange of girls in marriage and the recruitment and/or abduction of children for sexual exploitation. In these cases, UNODC suggests the existence of small core criminal organizations whose members maintain very high levels of secrecy, more because of fear of community outrage than through fear of detection by law enforcement, as they abduct children to be sold for sex trafficking (Kangaspunta, 2006). In addition, Estes and Weiner (2001) suggest that 20% of the children are trafficked through organized crime rings. With pimps and madams often receiving 80% or more of all monies made from the sexual abuse of their workforce, the incentive for the continued trafficking of children for sex is undeniable (Barnitz, 2000). In addition, as a trafficker can profit by thousands of dollars for supporting one child, it is expected that more and more children will become victims of sex trafficking in the United States and globally.

> Girls as young as thirteen are trafficked as mail-order brides (UNICEF, 2006).

Another emerging reason for the trafficking of individuals and specifically children is the desire for healthy internal organs. In 2003, it was reported that over the past decade, hundreds of women and children have been reported missing or murdered in the northern Mexican border town of Ciudad Juarez (Miles, 2003). It was speculated that one of the reasons for the murders was organ smuggling. In the United Kingdom, during the same period, a young Nigerian man's body was found with some of his organs missing. With the ever-pressing need for organs for transplantation in the United States and other developed countries, and fueled by the fear of AIDS in adults, a child is the perfect victim of human trafficking for internal organs. The child's organs are more likely to be healthy and HIV negative; thus, it is very profitable for those involved in trafficking and for those not deterred from murdering a child.

Finally, child soldiering and camel jockeying, although not documented to exist in the United States, are also reasons for the trafficking of children. It is not uncommon in developing countries for children to be kidnapped, their families bribed, or the families and/or children enticed through false promises of financial compensation into being trained as soldiers or to serve as camel jockeys (U.S. Department of State, 2004). Cases of child soldiering involve not only male children exploited for labor but also female children who are exploited sexually (Associated Press, 2007). In the United States, with various militia groups identified and the number increasing, particularly in the western parts of the country, it is not unlikely that children from underdeveloped countries will be trafficked into this country to be trained in combat.

How Children Are Trafficked

The trafficking of children, with perhaps the exception of family adoption, is essentially a financial investment. A single trafficked child can earn the trafficker up to $30,000, and, if many children are trafficked, the profits can be huge (Estes & Weiner, 2001). According to the UNODC, traffickers often target children because of their mental immaturity, their respect for adults as authority figures, and their poverty (Kangaspunta, 2006). In the United States and outside of the United States, children generally listen to and obey adults; hence, the adult trafficker is in a position of advantage when he or she captures the child. In addition, the family of the trafficked child has often sold that child or encouraged him or her to seek employment in a foreign country without knowledge of the work the child will be doing (Farr, 2004).

Child trafficking for sexual exploitation (the most common reason) is fueled by the thrill of having sex with a child and the fear of AIDS (Mirkinson, 1997). A virgin girl is valued at two to three times the price for a nonvirgin, and the supply from less developed countries seems endless (Armentrout, 2002). Of course, one cannot discount internal sex trafficking within the United States; the Department of Justice's Child Exploitation and Obscenity Section reports that cases involving girls from California as well as from Detroit have surfaced within the past few years (Richard, 1999). In both these cases, the young girls were trafficked into prostitution by members of their own ethnic communities and forced into sexual slavery. Finally, there currently exist approximately twenty-five companies in the United States known to operate sex tours for their clients (Andrews, 2004). It is not uncommon for some of these prostituted individuals to be under the age of eighteen. How the children actually enter the United States and are moved throughout the country is uncertain, although the common entry points into the United States for trafficking are beginning to be identified. Of course, false documentation is used in the majority of the cases.

In terms of child trafficking for sex, an immigrations investigation in Canada identified a human trafficking organization in Los Angeles responsible for trafficking American girls. Specifically, these girls were trafficked from the United States to Canada for prostitution (Richard, 1999). Therefore, although the United States is in most cases the destination country for child and adult trafficking, it can serve as the country of origin for trafficking, especially the trafficking of children.

Trafficking in children for labor also occurs in the United States; however, these cases typically involved African, Middle Eastern, or other non-American families bringing children from their native countries into the United States to work as domestic helps or as housekeepers (Richard, 1999). These trafficked children, in a similar situation to adults trafficked for domestic work, are forced to work long hours, are not allowed to attend school, receive little or no pay, and live in prison-like conditions. Of course, these cases are not limited to international families living in the United States, as Americans as well as church ministers have been identified in recent years as having forced children into the labor of cleaning, construction, and/or restaurant work (Richard, 1999).

Trafficked children follow similar routes to trafficked adults. However, most research suggests that children's routes into illegal activities are more cautious and specifically arranged before they ever leave their home countries (Somerset, 2001). As stated, in most cases, children are accompanied by an adult (often playing the role of their mother or father) or under the pretext of visiting a family member already living in the United States. By air, the most common points of entry are the international airports. For those individuals flying from London (Heathrow or Gatwick airports), the most common points of entry are Atlanta and New York (Somerset, 2004). In particular, New York City has been identified as a major point of entry and a transit area for traffickers placing victims in New York City or circulating them to other cities across the country (Spangenberg, 2002), and the Office of Homeland Security recently identified the Atlanta airport as one of the most lacking in terms of security.

Children from countries to the west of the United States have most often entered the country via California under the guise of visiting a family member. Just as with trafficked adults entering the country through New York or California, once the child enters a major city, he or she is shuffled from one area to another, with victims of sexual abuse or forced labor moved every fifteen to thirty days to avoid detection by law enforcement (Spangenberg, 2002).

Trafficked children are not a homogeneous group. In fact, variations in terms of gender, class, race, age, nationality, and immigration status are related to demand, their cost, and the amount of risk their traffickers are willing to take (Davidson, 2005). The tracking or identification of a child victim, once he or she begins the shuffle associated with trafficking in the United States, is nearly impossible. The children, often in the same situation as trafficked adults, are unable to speak English, are unable to seek help from Americans, and are subjected to repeated victimization. In addition, the children are often more profitable and easier to obtain.

> To prevent the detection of trafficking, traffickers move the children to a new location regularly (Spangenberg, 2002).

Why Child Trafficking Continues

Explanations as to why child trafficking continues go beyond the conditions of the countries of origin; however, it is suggested that recent economic crises in Asia and other countries have made children particularly vulnerable to traffickers as more and more children are leaving (or not allowed to attend) school and seeking employment (Richard, 1999). Another reason is the lack of awareness programs that focus on the demand for the sexual services of children (ECPAT-USANews, 2007). In many cases, the U.S. public is not aware of the fact that some individuals seek and enjoy sexual relationships with children or that individuals will force a child into laboring condition deemed unfit for an adult. Without this basic knowledge, there is no thought to begin the design and implementation of programs to educate the public.

The growth of child pornography is another explanation for the increase in child trafficking (McCabe, 2003). Online child pornography fuels the demand for child victims, and child pornography and trafficking is a gateway to the victims of these types of sexual exploitation (McCabe, 2007). As it becomes easier to identify and contact children via the Internet, it becomes easier for traffickers and those interested in the exploitation of children to identify a potential victim.

Finally, recent U.S. legislation has expanded the penalties for those who profit by human trafficking and specifically child trafficking; however, further legislation is needed to provide support for these child victims of trafficking, including decriminalizing the minor and providing the additional services uniquely required by children (ECPAT-USANews, 2007). For example, child victims of human trafficking are different from adult victims in that they will require education and the supervision of an adult. The child victim of trafficking, depending on his or her age, may need the services typically provided in toddler care, medical and growth checkups, or remedial education. These services would not be required for adults and therefore care would be more expensive for the child victims of human trafficking. In addition to their physical and educational needs, child victims of human trafficking will require socialization, counseling, social services interventions, patience, and perhaps even mental health treatment to begin their acclimation into mainstream society.

When exploiters are hard-pressed and law enforcement begins targeting the perpetrators of child trafficking, the demand for trafficked children increases. The exploiters then refine the process of trafficking and become more difficult for law enforcement to identify (Campagne & Poffenberger, 1988). In the United States, the majority of the trafficked children are not U.S. citizens, and they are perceived by many of the country's citizens as having been given an opportunity for a better quality of life; thus, the public pressure to end child trafficking is not present.

Law enforcement agencies, because of limited reporting by the public, the child's fear of the police and of deportation, and the child's lack of English skills, are often unaware of child trafficking cases (Spangenberg, 2002). Without awareness, law enforcement cannot act. Finally, child victims are somewhat difficult cases for law enforcement as the demographic characteristics of age is related to sanction and age changes. For example, a fourteen-year-old who is trafficked into the United States, abused for four years, then released and decides (on her own) to continue living in the United States until she is arrested for prostitution at the age of eighteen. Is this young woman a trafficking victim or a prostitute (Davidson, 2005)? The boundaries and definitions are not clear.

Profile of Countries and Traffickers

International trafficking, especially sex trafficking, of children between the ages of ten and fifteen is one of the largest segments of the global trade of people (Mirkinson, 1997). Most of the children involved in child trafficking are from Asia, Africa, Central and South America, and Central and Eastern Europe (Estes & Weiner, 2001). In fact, India alone has reported approximately 500,000 children involved in prostitution (Chidley, Wilhelmina, & Chu, 1996). For example, a 2004 advertisement in India lists 300 orphans aged between three and ten for sale (*Times of India*, 2005). U.K. officials report that between 5,000 and 10, 000 unaccompanied children arrive in their country annually, with some of these children planning to continue their travel into the United States (Somerset, 2001). As suggested, the key characteristics of the source countries are that they suffer from extreme poverty and repression, especially the repression of women, as is the case in third world countries, and therefore are easy targets for traffickers (King, 2004). These characteristics do not differ from the conditions facilitating adult trafficking.

The trafficker is most often perceived as a young, rich, and good-looking man; however, this is not always the case. Just as with the trafficking of adults, traffickers of children may be male or female, and the younger the children, the more often a woman (because of a gender-biased perception of love and mothering) is involved. These women, in cases of child trafficking, occupy the position of mother or caregiver in travel with the children to gain entry into the country. Once the children are in the county, the women often continue their day-to-day care until the children are moved to other caregivers or are killed because of their abusive situations. There have also been cases identified in which babies are taken or purchased from their families, raised to the age of five or six, and then trafficked for either sex or labor.

Those involved as clients of trafficked children are not always men, as many child domestics will report to and be controlled by women (Barnitz, 2000). Traffickers, especially those involved in the trafficking of children, have become increasingly flexible in adapting to situations and may change faces or appearances to allow the use of different travel routes to avoid detection (Lazaroiu & Alexandru, 2003). Customers seeking a child will search through word of mouth, existing brothels, phone booth advertisements, and Internet chat rooms (Somerset, 2001). Police often patrol well-known street prostitute areas; however, it is rare that a trafficked child will be identified in these areas. This ability of the traffickers to adjust their plans, along with their often-decentralized modes of transporting individuals, creates a very difficult environment for detection. The movement of victims from one trafficker to another allows changes of defense by the traffickers in response to the latest police efforts (Van Impe, 2000). Without the centrality of leadership and control often found in adult trafficking operations and historically in organized crime, the individual traffickers involved in child trafficking are among the most important elements in the activity (Skeldon, 2000). Traffickers may pose as a family member, a friend to the child, an adopting adult, or the head of a modeling agency, and all within the role of trafficking the child (Lazaroiu & Alexandru, 2003). The home country does not miss the child, the traffickers are organized, and work in the United States is ideal. Traffickers to the United States are encouraged by large tax-free profits, the continued income from the same victim, and the relatively minor penalties; therefore, child trafficking continues (Miko, 2004).

Proactive and Reactive U.S. Legislative Measures

In 2003, the United States strengthened its role in fighting human trafficking by passing legislation specifically to fight child sex tourism (U.S. Department of State, 2005). The PROTECT Act increases penalties for those involved in child sex tourism to a maximum of thirty years in prison. Since the PRO-TECT Act there have been more than twenty indictments and more than a dozen convictions (U.S. Department of State, 2005). This measure, along with the various states passing laws against forced child labor and child sexual exploitation, demonstrates the commitment by the United States to end child trafficking, because now, in some states, convicted traffickers face a minimum of twenty-five years in prison (*Crime Control Digest*, 2006). In addition, the Department of Homeland Security has developed Operation Predator to combat child exploitation, child pornography, and child sex tourism. Finally, in Cancún, Mexico, the hottest destination for American tourists in Mexico, training and awareness efforts on the subject of child trafficking have been introduced to hotel staff and U.S. tourists (ECPAT, 2007).

It is now realized by U.S. law enforcement and government officials that child trafficking may be addressed only through national and international efforts. The United Nations Protocol to Prevent, Suppress, and Punish Trafficking in Persons, especially Women and Children, is an international agreement to address human trafficking, especially the trafficking of children on an international level (Ejalu, 2006). It creates the global language necessary to define trafficking in persons, assist victims, and prevent trafficking. Also within the protocol, parameters for judicial cooperation and exchanges of information among countries are intended to facilitate the establishment of laws and synchronized legislation across borders.

To reduce the number of incidents of child trafficking, the U.S. government has supported several research initiatives focusing on sexual exploitation. Specifically, in 2006, the Office of Juvenile Justice and Delinquency Prevention announced a $1.3 million effort to study the sexual exploitation of children through trafficking and prostitution. In addition, juvenile justice officials have developed a number of prevention and intervention programs focused on assisting these exploited children (*Corrections Digest*, 2006).

Summary

The trafficking of children is another aspect of human trafficking that has gained global attention in the past few years. Child trafficking occurs for many reasons, including labor, adoption, drug smuggling, sex, and the trade in healthy internal organs. Unfortunately, the extent of child trafficking in the United States is unknown as there exists no national system for tracking unaccompanied minors within or outside of the United States.

The trafficking of children is essentially a financial investment. A single trafficked child can earn the trafficker up to $30,000, and many times the family of the trafficked child has no knowledge of the child's abuse. The most common reason for child trafficking is sexual exploitation. Trafficked children follow the same travel routes into the United States as trafficked adults; however, most research suggests that the child's route into illegal activities is more cautious than the adult's route and specifically arranged before the child ever leaves his or her home country.

Trafficked children vary by gender, race, and age, with these characteristics influencing the demand for them and their traffickers' profits. To address child trafficking for sexual exploitation, the U.S. government has passed the PRO-TECT Act, which increases penalties for those involved in child sex tourism to a maximum of thirty years in prison. In addition, the Department of Homeland Security has launched Operation Predator to combat child exploitation, child pornography, and child sex tourism. Finally, funding has been made available to support proactive programs to address child trafficking.

Questions on Chapter 5

1. What are the reasons for child trafficking?
2. Why are children often easier targets of human trafficking than adults?
3. Are there any common characteristics among trafficked children?
4. How do traffickers target or identify the child victims for human trafficking? Why are the parents of trafficked children not demanding the return of their children?
5. What are the responses within the United States and abroad to the criminal action of child trafficking?

Questions for Further Thought

1. Given the conditions that exist for most of the victims of child trafficking in their country of origin, isn't their life better in the United States?
2. If a child chooses to be trafficked to the United States to help his or her family, should we be concerned about his or her victimization?

3. As law enforcement efforts rarely focus on trafficked children, does legislation really make a difference?
4. If a child is trafficked into the United States and remains in the United States for many years by his or her own choice, is he or she still a victim of human trafficking?
5. If law enforcement does not make child trafficking a priority, is the legislation meaningless?

NATIONAL AND INTERNATIONAL
EFFORTS

In the United States there are more and more cases of individuals being held against their will to work as domestics or nannies or farm workers (found locked inside barracks and working under armed guard as field slaves) and of children being prostituted (Bales, 2004). Given an average salary of $25 per month in the countries of the former Soviet Union (Junger, 2002) and the philosophy that trafficking people is less risky than trafficking drugs or arms (Kelly & Regan, 2000), the trafficking of humans is expected to continue unless efforts are made to end this criminal activity.

One of the first problems that must be acknowledged when addressing human trafficking is the definition itself. Human trafficking refers to a number of practices and consequences, not one single act leading to a specific outcome (O'Connell-Davidson, 2002). The ambiguity of this phrase leads to confusion not only in the identification of cases but also in the enforcement of laws against human trafficking. Despite the vagueness of definition, the United States is recognized as a primary destination country for individuals trafficked from other countries. These victims are believed to come from countries within Asia, the former Soviet Union, Eastern Europe, and Mexico (Miko, 2004).

The U.S. government has attempted to address the problem of definition in its focus on phenomena such as domestic violence and hate crimes; however, as the majority of the U.S. victims of trafficking are not U.S. citizens and human trafficking seems, at best, far removed from the public's concern, the legal community is very much at a disadvantage when attempting to address human trafficking victims or its perpetrators. What must be recognized and communicated is the outcome—that human trafficking produces a new form of slavery in the United States.

Specifically, through human trafficking, chattel slavery, in which a person is captured, born, or sold into permanent servitude, exists (Bales, 2004). Through human trafficking, debt bondage (the most common outcome from trafficking for labor) and contract slavery (which involves the use of a contract to assure "employment,") now also exist (Bales, 2004). Of course, this assurance of employment is of minimal benefit to the victim and maximum benefit to the trafficker.

The second problem that must be acknowledged when addressing human trafficking is that there has been no method for collecting information on the cases of trafficking (Campagne & Poffenberger, 1988). Of course, this changed in 2000 with the Trafficking Victims Protection Act (TVPA). However, little is known about current-day human trafficking in this country and forecasts of long-term trends are imprecise. Until recently, human trafficking cases have been identified through reports from law enforcement or through a few select nongovernmental organizations (NGOs), a count of the number of prostitutes working in a given district, and surveys. Through governmental efforts to identify the incidence and prevalence of these cases, and in cooperation with NGOs, a better picture of human trafficking is now being captured.

Finally, a problem that must be acknowledged when addressing human trafficking is that not only adults but also children are involved. Although it may be acceptable for an adult to be involved in prostitution, minors cannot legally consent to sex with adults in the United States; however, most people assume that those under the age of eighteen who are involved in sexual exploitation choose to be involved, and the same sentiment often applies to those trafficked for sexual exploitation. Because of the blurred jurisdictional lines between U.S. law enforcement and social services, the perceived "turf wars" between governmental agencies and NGOs, and the fact that some researchers and practitioners argue that children are not prostitutes but victims of sexual abuse (Somerset, 2001), it is difficult to determine the number of child victims of human trafficking or to determine specific demographic characteristics of those victims. This problem is not unique to the United States. Other countries with conflicting agencies with responsibility and variability in the definition of a child have difficulties in obtaining accurate figures on the number of children involved in human trafficking (Melrose, 2002).

National Laws and Programs

During the twentieth century, there was no single department or agency responsible for collecting data on human trafficking or those offenses relating to trafficking. In 1998, the U.S. government estimated that between 45,000 and 50,000 people were trafficked into the United States annually (U.S. Department of Justice, 2003a). Surprisingly, it was not public opinion or human rights groups but big business concerns about labor competition that prompted the awareness of human trafficking in this country (Bales, 2004). Competition and the notion that employers with trafficked employees could complete the work at a fraction of the cost pressed the capitalist system of the United States to begin efforts to eliminate human trafficking. By 2003, the estimate of individuals trafficked into the United States had been reduced to between 18,000 and 20,000 (U.S. Department of Justice, 2003a).

After Secretary of State Colin Powell announced that monies acquired through human trafficking were used to support the 9/11 hijackers while they lived in this country, public opinion and government efforts began to acknowledge the phenomenon. Legislative and police efforts were initiated to recognize human trafficking as not only a humanitarian interest but also an issue of national security.

> Trafficking Victims Protection Act of 2000 (P.L. 106-386, H.R. 3244).
> Trafficking Victims Protection Reauthorization Act of 2003 (H.R. 2620).
> Trafficking Victims Protection Reauthorization Act of 2005 (H.R. 972).

The 2000 TVPA, signed by President Clinton, established the Office to Monitor and Combat Trafficking in Persons, in Washington, DC. In February 2002, President Bush signed an Executive Order to establish an Interagency Task Force to include the secretary of state, the attorney general, the secretary of labor, the secretary of health and human services, and the director of the Central Intelligence Agency (CIA). The task force was charged with strengthening the coordination efforts among agencies and identifying the needs of trafficking victims, punishing traffickers, and preventing trafficking in future (Miko, 2004). The 2000 TVPA was amended and signed by President George W. Bush in 2003 as the Trafficking Victims Protection Reauthorization Act (TVPRA), which mandated responsibilities and duties regarding human trafficking to federal agencies, including the Department of State, the Department of Labor, and the Department of Health and Human Services.

The TVPRA, signed again in 2005 (H.R. 972), provides tools to combat trafficking in persons both worldwide and domestically. Therefore, in addition to the TVPA's requirements to provide victim assistance, to define new crimes and penalties, and to assist foreign countries in drafting their laws against human trafficking, federal agencies were now sharing the responsibility to reduce and eliminate human trafficking. For example, according to a law passed in September 2002, to better inform women about and protect them against abuse and forced prostitution, foreign-born women may request to view their fiancés' criminal history before leaving their country for the United States (Crandall et al., 2005). Of course, viewing this information is not mandatory, and many women in the mail-order bride industry are not aware this information is available.

> The 2000 Trafficking Victims Protection Act (TVPA) established the Office to Monitor and Combat Trafficking in Persons.

Since 2002, the Department of Justice has aggressively prosecuted human trafficking offenders, and the Department of Health and Human Services continues to provide medical services, shelter, and counseling to the victims. The Department of Justice's trafficking caseload doubled between 2001 and 2003. According to the Department of State, as of January 2003 approximately 450 trafficking victims had benefited from these newly created provisions. To better inform the public and victims, the departments of Labor, Justice, and Health and Human Services have developed brochures for NGOs to distribute that identify the signs of human trafficking (U.S. Department of State, 2003b). By 2002, approximately 200 international anti-trafficking programs were being funded in countries around the globe (U.S. Department of State, 2003c). The U.S. Office to Monitor and Combat Trafficking in Persons annually reports human rights practices with regard to human trafficking by country. In addition, hotlines have been established to report victims of human trafficking.

Among its proactive approaches to eliminate human trafficking, the Department of Homeland Security established its Operation Predator program to help protect children from becoming victims of international sex tourism and traffickers (U.S. Department of State, 2004) and immigration officials warn people about the dangers of purchasing products made by trafficked labor at the land borders of the United States (U.S. Department of State, 2003b).

The U.S. Department of Justice, in addition to holding its first trafficking-specific training for law enforcement and other federal agencies in June 2004, has continued its training of enforcement officers and supported anti-trafficking task forces in Philadelphia, Atlanta, and Phoenix.

To further support the international community in the fight against human trafficking, the departments of State and Justice are training foreign law enforcement and immigration officers around the globe to identify the victims of human trafficking and the traffickers. In addition, the United States hosted the 2003 conference "Pathbreaking Strategies in the Global Fight against Sex Trafficking" and works with the European Union, the United Nations, and other international organizations to support anti-trafficking programs in more than seventy-five countries (Miko, 2004). Finally, the U.S. government engages with countries internationally that supports the United Nations Optional Protocol to Prevent, Suppress, and Punish those responsible for trafficking in persons and has initiated programs in a number of countries, including Russia and the Philippines (Miko, 2004).

To demonstrate the United States' concern to maintain attention on the activity of human trafficking, in September 2005, the U.S. Congress requested follow-up information from President Bush regarding the support provided by the United States to foreign countries and NGOs within those countries and on progress in creating human trafficking laws and providing services to trafficking victims.

International Programs and Best Practices

On the international front, there have been, and continue to be, multiple efforts to reduce or eliminate human trafficking. NGOs such as the Global Survival Network and Human Rights Watch are leaders in their attempts to raise awareness and reduce incidents of human trafficking outside of U.S. borders (Farr, 2004). In addition, governmental organizations such as the International Labour Organization (ILO) are committed to helping child victims of commercial sexual exploitation, often through trafficking (Barnitz, 2000), and the United Nations held a convention in December 2003 on transnational organized crime, including those organized criminal units involved in organized human trafficking (Munro, 2006).

Countries such as the United Kingdom have begun to identify victims of trafficking, including children, and to determine the reasons behind the trafficking, such as prostitution, labor, and the fact that male children are often exploited to obtain financial benefits from social service agencies (Somerset, 2004). It has been suggested that nearly 80% of the prostitutes within the London brothels are foreign (Bell, 2001). In addition, the United Kingdom has established a checklist of observations and questions to assist in establishing the identities of adults traveling with children. The following brief descriptions of anti-trafficking initiatives include the "best practices" of some of the countries classified within the tier system.

Australia

Australia is a destination country for a small number of trafficking cases and is a leader in the fight against human trafficking. In 2003, the Australian government announced a $20-million effort to measure and combat human trafficking. In 2004, the government strengthened its legislation against human trafficking by further defining the actions involved in trafficking and increasing the penalties for those convicted of human trafficking. Also in 2004, the Australian Federal Police's Transnational Sexual Exploitation and Trafficking Team was charged with distinguishing trafficking victims from smuggled individuals. The Australian government not only funds and coordinates anti-trafficking efforts in Australia but also funds trafficking awareness and prevention programs in source countries. Finally, Australia's Crime Act is used to prosecute and convict Australian citizens who travel internationally for the purpose of having sex with a person under the age of sixteen. Australia has been classified as a Tier 1 country for several years.

Austria

Austria, a Tier 1 country since 2004, is a transit and destination country for human trafficking, with most of the victims coming from countries such as Poland, Romania, and Nigeria. Although Austria does not provide the most accurate records on the number of trafficking cases, it is suggested that approximately two-thirds of the victims of human trafficking are trafficked for sexual exploitation and the remaining one-third for forced labor. Police in Austria also estimate that much of the human trafficking is controlled by crime organizations primarily from Eastern Europe. Most of the victims trafficked to Austria are brought to the country under false promises of waitress or nanny jobs. Austria's Criminal Law Amendment Act of 2004 targets human trafficking with specific legislation and penalties for those convicted of trafficking.

Belgium

Belgium, a Tier 1 country in 2004, is a transit and destination country for human trafficking. Belgium's victims are trafficked for both sex and labor, and many are natives of countries such as Nigeria, Albania, and China. The Brussels Declaration of 2003 was created to mandate the assessment of measures against trafficking. Through this declaration, European and international cooperation will be developed to establish concrete measures, standards, and best practices to prevent and combat human trafficking. Victims of sexual exploitation were increasingly women under the age of eighteen, and victims of forced labor were often young Chinese men. At one time, there was a huge involvement of Albanian gangs in human trafficking in Belgium; however, officials report that Albanian gang activity has decreased in the country over the past few years because of targeted efforts to reduce human trafficking.

Canada

Canada, a Tier 1 country for several years, is a destination for human trafficking, with victims arriving from all corners of the world, including Eastern Europe and Asia. Many of the victims of human trafficking in Canada are children. Since 2002, Canada's Cybertip.com has existed as an online tip line dedicated to ending the sexual exploitation of children, including human trafficking for sexual exploitation. On Cybertip, the top five risks children face while on the Internet as well as signs of child sexual exploitation are posted. In the fall of 2007, Cybertip led to twenty-three arrests and the identification of more than 15,000 Web sites intended to victimize children (ECPAT, 2007).

Colombia

Colombia, a Tier 1 country in 2004, is a major source country for victims trafficked all over the world, including to the countries of Latin America and the United States. Although Colombian men are trafficked for forced labor, the majority of their victims are women and girls. Organized crime units, some connected to terrorist organizations, are involved with the trafficking of persons. Children are especially vulnerable in Colombia as many drop out of school and then are targeted (sometimes kidnapped) for victimization. Colombian authorities have recognized their problem of human trafficking and are attempting to fund educational and awareness efforts to the general public. Funds are received annually from other countries to reduce the problem of human trafficking and the Colombian government has responded with more legislation targeting those who victimize residents through human trafficking.

Czech Republic

Although the Czech Republic is economically one of the most stable countries within central and Eastern Europe, it has been identified as a source, transit, and destination country for human trafficking. The Czech Republic, a Tier 1 country in 2004, is a transit and destination country for women from areas such as Russia, the Ukraine, and China and is a source country for women trafficked to countries such as Germany and Austria. It is a destination country for individuals trafficked from countries such as India and North Korea for forced labor. In fact, the Czech Republic suggests that forced labor is among the types of human trafficking increasing most. In 2002, the Czech Republic began an aggressive campaign of awareness targeting the general public on the dangers of human trafficking for prostitution. Also within the Czech Republic are campaigns to increase awareness on the subject of child trafficking as related to both sexual exploitation and the internal trafficking of children for labor.

Denmark

Denmark, a Tier 1 country in 2004, is a transit and destination country for sex trafficking. The majority of the victims are from countries such as the Ukraine, the Baltic states, Thailand, and Nigeria. Danish authorities suggest that a strong link exists between organized crime (especially Russian gangs) and human trafficking. Awareness and education programs, for the most part started around 2002, focus on the problem of child sex trafficking as legislation now exists that carries stiff penalties for those convicted of trafficking children for sexual exploitation.

France

France is a destination country for women and girls trafficked for sexual exploitation. The majority of these victims are from countries such as Romania, Albania, and Nigeria. France's government suggests that the majority of the women in the commercial sex trade are from countries other than France and are victims of sex trafficking. In the past few years, and in response to the number of trafficking victims, France, a Tier 1 country in 2004, launched and has continued to implement aggressive awareness programs to provide victims of sex trafficking information on assistance available to them. In addition, the government has enacted legislation with severe penalties for those found guilty of sex trafficking. France is now beginning to address trafficking for forced labor, as it now suggests that 20% of its involuntary domestic servitude cases involve employers who are diplomats.

Germany

The Federal Republic of Germany is a transit and destination country for sex and labor trafficking. Victims of both sex and labor trafficking are from countries such as Romania, Bulgaria, and Africa. Unique to Germany, a Tier 1 country in 2004, among its systems attempting to count the number of victims of human trafficking is the identification of the gender, age, and nationality of victims. Germany suggests that a significant number of its victims of human trafficking are victims of internal trafficking and that approximately 10% of the victims of sex trafficking are children. Germany also suggests that more than half of the child victims of sex trafficking are natives of the country.

Ghana

The Republic of Ghana is a source, transit, and destination country for sex and labor trafficking. Much of the human trafficking is done internally, especially when the victims are male. Young boys from Ghana, a Tier 1 country in 2004, are trafficked for forced labor in the fishing industry, in agriculture, and in mines. Girls are trafficked internally and externally for domestic servitude and sexual exploitation. During the first five months of 2005, Ghana's government reported that in more than one-half of its cases involving child trafficking, the children were kidnapped from their homes. In the remaining cases, it was not unusual for parents to give or sell their children to traffickers. As child trafficking is a major concern for Ghana's government, awareness and prevention efforts have focused on the children and their parents. More severe penalties now exist for those found guilty of selling a child or trafficking a child for exploitation.

Hong Kong

Hong Kong, a Tier 1 country in 2004, is a transit and destination country for human trafficking for both sex and labor. Many of the victims are from

China and Southeast Asia. Although Hong Kong has no specific laws against trafficking, a range of criminal offenses are used to prosecute those involved in trafficking. Hong Kong's government devotes numerous resources to monitoring trafficking and to collecting data on human trafficking cases. The government also has strong controls in labor and manufacturing industries that monitor for victims of labor trafficking. Hong Kong provides a range of social services to identified victims of human trafficking and its Security Bureau oversees the training of police and immigration officials in the recognition of trafficking cases and in interviewing victims of human trafficking.

India

India, ranked as a Tier 2 Watch country in 2004, is a source, destination, and transit country for adults and children. It is estimated that the number of individuals trafficked within or through India is in the millions, with many of those victims being children. In India, approximately 25% of the population lives below the poverty line and approximately 400 million are under the age of eighteen. Traffickers are aware that these conditions facilitate human trafficking and utilize these conditions to their advantage. Women and children are trafficked out of the country for both sex and labor. India is a destination country for trafficking victims from countries such as Nepal and Bangladesh and a transit country for victims en route to Pakistan and other countries within the Middle East.

In addition, government officials suggest that 90% of India's trafficking is internal. Trafficked children are often found working in carpet manufacturing and the silk industry throughout the country. Women are also found to be victims of labor and sex trafficking. In response to the widespread occurrence of human trafficking within India, the Joint Women's Programme, in collaboration with other NGOs, has provided gender-sensitive training for police to be better able to assist women and girls who have been victims of violence and trafficking (Banerjee, 2006).

In addition, according to government reports, there are more than eighty NGOs in India today working to reduce human trafficking. These organizations, focused mainly on sex trafficking, respond to the unique conditions in their areas in various ways. For example, in Madhya Pradesh, an organization called Abhyudaya Ashram works with both police and social service agents to identify and support victims of sex trafficking as well as offer them an education through the residential school system (Banerjee, 2006). Another organization, in Calcutta, has been involved in providing training on women's rights and legal protection to victims of sex trafficking, with much of this training focused on stopping the influx of young girls into sex trafficking. Finally, other organizations such as Prerna in Mumbai are involved in not only the rehabilitation of victims of sex trafficking but also actively lobbying state governments for assistance with victims and harsher penalties for those convicted of sex trafficking (Banerjee, 2006).

Israel

In 2004, Israel was categorized as a Tier 2 country as it is a destination country for workers from countries such as China, India, and Eastern Europe. These trafficking victims are often forced into domestic servitude, construction, or agricultural work. According to government reports, women in the health care field are especially vulnerable to trafficking for forced labor.

In Israel, it is suggested that organized crime groups traffic women from Eastern Europe into Israel for prostitution and other forms of sexual exploitation. In fact, it is estimated that of the 200,000 foreign workers in Israel, 20% are victims of human trafficking.

In response to Israel's problem with human trafficking, the Isha L'Isha project in northern Israel was established in 2002 to provide public support to women victims and to raise awareness of the phenomenon of trafficking women (Chaikin, 2006). Since the inception of Isha, public awareness on human trafficking has increased, a legislative committee has been established, and law enforcement agencies are inviting representatives from Isha to discuss the signs and problems associated with human trafficking (Beeks & Amir, 2006). More than eighty women have been provided assistance since the first year of the project. Isha L'Isha decided to focus on the two goals of providing support for women victims of sex trafficking and raising public awareness of human trafficking. The support for women victims has included emotional, social, medical, and legal support and arrangements for the return of victims (if they desire) to their home countries.

In addition, Isha representatives have participated in numerous national and international workshops focused on human trafficking and have created information brochures, in various languages, to provide victims a source for contact if they choose to ask for help. Finally, as a result of Isha's efforts, the government opened a shelter for victims of sex trafficking willing to testify in court against their traffickers (Chaikin, 2006).

Italy

On the basis of 2004 and 2005 *TIP* reports, Italy is classified as a Tier 1 country and is a transit and destination country for adults and children trafficked for both sex and labor. The majority of the women and children trafficked into Italy are from countries such as Nigeria, Romania, and the Ukraine. The majority of the men trafficked into Italy are trafficked for forced labor in the agricultural sector and are predominantly from either Poland or China. It is suggested that approximately 10% of Italy's trafficking victims are children and that many of the human trafficking victims are en route to other parts of Europe, South America, or North America.

The government of Italy has recognized the high rates of unemployment and trafficking within the country and has implemented programs to curtail the problems. Specifically, Project Textilia 2000 provides gainful employment to prevent victims from being trafficked. As Project Textilia recognizes that poverty and oppression are key factors in human trafficking, through the provision of employment, individuals who may be targets for traffickers are given options.

Lithuania

Lithuania, a Tier 1 country in 2004, is a source, transit, and destination country for women and children trafficked for sexual exploitation. Of these victims, approximately one-third are children. Lithuanians are trafficked to Germany, Italy, Spain, and the United Kingdom. In 2002, the Lithuanian government began to implement a program focused on the Control and Prevention of Human Trafficking and Prostitution. It is suggested that organized crime is behind much of the human trafficking and that these organized crime groups are both from Lithuania and from other countries. As the Lithuanian government has acknowledged its problem of human trafficking, the public as well as law enforcement are being trained on signs of human trafficking. Recent legislative efforts have made the trafficking of persons (and especially children) an offense punishable by a significant prison sentence.

Macedonia

The Republic of Macedonia, a Tier 1 country in 2004, is a source and transit country for human trafficking for sexual exploitation. Most recently, Macedonia has also been recognized as a destination country for some cases of sex trafficking. Macedonian women and children are trafficked within the country and to countries such as Germany, Spain, and the United Kingdom. Victims are trafficked through Macedonia to countries such as Serbia, Albania, and the countries of Western Europe. The Macedonian government has established a Trafficking of Children subgroup as well as programs to provide shelter for victims of human trafficking in cooperation with nongovernmental agencies. The government has also committed to prevent and combat transborder crime and trafficking within neighboring countries. Finally, the Macedonian government operates a Task Force for Human Trafficking, which is responsible for designing and implementing countrywide efforts to end human trafficking.

Morocco

The Kingdom of Morocco is a source, transit, and destination country for human trafficking. In particular, Morocco is a source country for children trafficked internally for labor in terms of domestic servitude and a source, transit, and destination country for women and children trafficked for sexual exploitation. Destinations for those trafficked from and through Morocco include Saudi Arabia, Syria, and Western Europe. As Moroccan authorities have discovered that many child victims of human trafficking are sold by their parents, legislative efforts have increased the penalties for those selling children and awareness efforts are underway to educate the public on the plight of victims of human trafficking. Morocco was a Tier 1 country in 2004.

The Netherlands

The Netherlands, a Tier 1 country in 2004, is a source, transit, and destination country for both sex and labor trafficking. Internally, women and girls are trafficked for sexual exploitation. In addition, women and children are trafficked to and through the Netherlands from countries such as Nigeria, Poland, and China for sex. To some extent, men and young boys are also trafficked to countries such as India and Turkey, a Tier 1 country in 2004, for forced labor in the fishing industry, for factory work, and for restaurant help. The Netherlands authorities report that approximately 25% of the victims of human trafficking were living in the country when they were recruited for human trafficking. In response, during the past few years, governmental and nongovernmental efforts have focused on awareness of human trafficking and victim assistance programs for those already involved in the sex industry.

New Zealand

New Zealand, a Tier 1 country for several years, is a destination country for women trafficked from Thailand and other countries within Southeast Asia. The majority of New Zealand's victims are victims of sexual exploitation. Although prostitution is legal in New Zealand, it is illegal for nonnatives to work in the commercial sex industry. In 2004, the New Zealand government acknowledged an abundance of minors working within the sex industry and efforts to reduce this phenomenon were implemented. The government provides support for NGOs offering services such as shelter, medical assistance, and counseling for victims of human trafficking. In 2006, the government also implemented a plan to target those involved in child trafficking that included severe penalties for those committing child sex offenses in other countries.

Norway

The Kingdom of Norway, a Tier 1 country for several years, is a transit and destination country for victims of human trafficking. Norway is rich in natural resources and is also economically prosperous; thus traffickers target Norway for the best profits from their victims. Victims within Norway are from countries such as Nigeria, Russia, and Estonia, and most are victims of sex trafficking. Those victims trafficked through Norway often are en route to countries such as Italy or Sweden. Aware of its problem of sex trafficking, the government of Norway has implemented several anti-trafficking programs as well as increased legislative efforts to end human trafficking.

Panama

Panama, ranked as a Tier 2 country for several years, is a source, transit, and destination country for sex and labor trafficking. Women and children are trafficked from countries such as Peru, China, Colombia, and the Dominican Republic for sexual exploitation and through Panama en route to countries such as Jamaica, other Central American countries, and the United States. Government officials in Panama have acknowledged that a large number of children are trafficked internally for sexual exploitation through sex tourism and forced labor.

In response to the problem of child trafficking, the government of Panama enacted a new anti-trafficking law in 2004 that seeks to address the child pornography and sex tourism outcomes of human trafficking. Under this law, airlines, tour agencies, and hotels are mandated to inform their customers about the new law. Also under this law, the Technical Judicial Police (PTJ: Policía Técnica Judicial) investigated trafficking cases for prosecution by the Attorney General's Office.

The Philippines

The Philippines is a source, transit, and destination country for adult and child victims of human trafficking. In 2004, the Philippines was ranked within the Tier 2 Watch category. Adults and children trafficked for both sex and labor are en route to countries such as Saudi Arabia, Kuwait, Europe, and North America. Women and children trafficked into the Philippines are from countries such as China, South Korea, and Russia. Individuals trafficked within the country are often trafficked from the poorer rural areas to the urban areas for forced labor in domestic servitude, commercial sexual exploitation, and the drug trade. Within the Philippines, children are also trafficked for the purpose of sexual abuse and for work in the drug trade.

The Philippines ranks fourth among the worst nine nations with problems of prostitution and sexual exploitation with anywhere from 60,000 to 100,000 individuals involved in prostitution and trafficking (Jurado, 2005). To address the problem, awareness and assessment programs have been implemented and supported by a delegation of representatives from the European Union (Jurado, 2005). In addition, to target human trafficking for labor in the Philippines, the government conducts periodic checks of labor markets to ensure the legality of their workers and Philippine Foreign Service officials are trained and, in some cases, actively involved in searching housing units for trafficked individuals.

Finally, in May 2006, the Anti-Trafficking Bill, Republic Act 9208, was finally passed by the Philippine Congress and Senate. This Act treats human trafficking as a human rights violation, and the act of trafficking is subject to penalties because of the intention to profit from human slavery. In addition, this Act introduces standards for the protection of trafficking victims such as confidentiality, victim protection, closed-door trials, and funds to assist with a victim's reintegration into society (Ruiz-Austria, 2006).

Poland

The Republic of Poland, a Tier 1 country for several years, is a source, transit, and destination country for human trafficking. Many of the victims within Poland are from Russia, Bulgaria, and Vietnam and travel through Poland en route to Austria, Sweden, and Japan. The majority of the victims are used for sexual exploitation. Polish authorities are very aggressive in their pursuit of traffickers and have identified cases involving boys from Vietnam trafficked through Poland for forced labor and sexual exploitation. During 2006, Polish law enforcement identified more than 600 victims of human trafficking. Legislative efforts in Poland support the efforts of law enforcement, as those convicted of human trafficking, especially the trafficking of children, face significant prison terms.

Portugal

The Portuguese Republic, a Tier 1 country for several years, is primarily a transit and destination country for victims trafficked for sexual exploitation. The major source country for Portugal is Brazil, and Brazilian women and children are trafficked throughout Europe. Male victims within Portugal are often from Eastern Europe and are victims of labor trafficking in the construction industry. Governmental efforts to combat human trafficking have been significant in Portugal and include not only legislation prohibiting human trafficking and severe penalties for those convicted of human trafficking but also the provision of services to victims. These funded services to victims of human trafficking include medical services, counseling services, and job skills training.

Republic of Korea (South Korea)

South Korea, a Tier 1 country for several years, is a primary source country for the trafficking of women and girls internally and to the United States. Many of these victims enter the United States through Canada or Mexico. Increasingly, victims of human trafficking (women) outside Korea are brought into the country through marriage arrangements with Korean men. Once these marriages have ended, the women become victims of labor or sex trafficking. South Korean men also drive the market in demand for child trafficking for sexual exploitation. South Korea has begun programs to reduce internal trafficking and has increased the penalties for those convicted of human trafficking within the country.

Spain

Spain is primarily a destination country for women and children of the former Soviet Union, Nigeria, and the Middle East. Spain, a Tier 1 country for several years, recognizes the importance of awareness and education in its efforts to reduce human trafficking. The government of Spain has increased its legislation to combat human trafficking and has increased its penalties for those convicted of human trafficking, especially the trafficking of children for sexual exploitation.

In 2004, Madrid announced a comprehensive effort to combat prostitution and trafficking. This effort, using Sweden's well-established governmental model, is based on the principle that the best way to combat prostitution and trafficking is to target the customers.

Sweden

The Kingdom of Sweden, a Tier 1 country for several years, is a transit and destination country for human trafficking. Many of the victims of human trafficking in Sweden are victims of sexual exploitation and are from countries such as Hungary, Macedonia, and Russia. Sweden serves as a transit country for victims en route to Germany, Spain, and the United Kingdom. It is also a transit country for children from China to countries throughout Western Europe. Law enforcement and legislative efforts within Sweden are quite aggressive in their attempt to combat human trafficking. Most recently, police identified a new trend of children being trafficked from Eastern Europe into Sweden for the purposes of begging and petty larceny.

Taiwan

Taiwan, a Tier 1 country for several years, is both a transit and destination country for victims of sex and labor trafficking. The majority of the victims of human trafficking within the country are from China, Cambodia, and Vietnam. Taiwan is a primary transit country for victims of human trafficking en route to the United States. In addition, Taiwan has a significant number of victims of internal trafficking. The majority of the victims of human trafficking in Taiwan are victims of sex trafficking; however, labor trafficking is also a problem for both males and females. In addition to enacting strict laws prohibiting human trafficking, the Taiwanese authorities have increased their efforts to assist victims and in 2004 piloted a program for assistance to Vietnamese victims of sexual exploitation. Currently, law enforcement and immigration officials attempt to interview every identified illegal alien to determine he or she is a victim of human trafficking. Police are trained to recognize patterns of human trafficking and to handle victims of trafficking. Finally, the Taiwanese government has begun to implement awareness programs aimed at the use of the Internet for the sexual exploitation of minors. Included in this focus are those perpetrators using the Internet to promote child trafficking.

Thailand

Thailand was ranked as a Tier 2 Watch country in 2004 and is a source, transit, and destination country for adults and children trafficked for sex and labor. Victims from countries such as Burma, Laos, and China are trafficked into the country. The destinations for many of the victims trafficked through Thailand are countries such as Malaysia, Japan, Canada, and the United States.

Government officials in Thailand estimate that there are approximately 250,000 sex workers within the country. In response, project EMPOWER is a needs- and rights-based model program to provide outreach in terms of education, training, counseling, and health services to sex workers and victims of sex trafficking (Banerjee, 2006).

Finally, Thailand's government has focused on providing special care and support for child victims of trafficking, preventing child trafficking, and facilitating the nonharmful involvement of child victims as witnesses in human trafficking trials (Gallagher, 2006).

The United Kingdom

The United Kingdom of Great Britain and Northern Ireland, a Tier 1 country for several years, is primarily a destination country for human trafficking. Victims within the United Kingdom are from countries such as Russia, Thailand, Africa, and Nigeria. Of course, victims are also trafficked within the United Kingdom. The majority of the victims within the United Kingdom are victims of sexual exploitation; however, children (particularly from African countries) are forced into labor within the factories of the United Kingdom. The United Kingdom has also been identified as a transit country for those victims en route to the United States for either sex or labor trafficking. The United Kingdom is especially aggressive in its efforts by government and NGOs to end child trafficking and sexual exploitation of children.

The United States

The U.S. government, although not ranked in 2006, estimates that approximately 50,000 individuals are trafficked into the country or through the country to work as sex slaves, in domestic servitude, or in the garment industry or agriculture. The United States is a source and destination country for adults and children from locations such as East Asia, Eastern Europe, Mexico, and Central America. Also in the United States there exist an unknown number of American citizens and legal residents trafficked within the country for sex and labor.

In response, the U.S. government continues to advance the goal of ending human trafficking within the country through coordinated federal and state efforts. In addition, the U.S. government allocated approximately $28 million toward domestic programs to boost anti-trafficking law enforcement efforts, to protect victims of human trafficking, and to raise awareness of human trafficking in the public arena.

Countries Not Ranked

To avoid ranking countries without clear evidence, the 2006 *TIP* did not classify within the tier system thirteen countries in addition to the United States because of incomplete, unclear, and/or contradictory information. The countries are the Bahamas, Barbados, Brunei, Haiti, Iraq, Ireland, Kiribati, Lesotho, Solomon Islands, Somalia, Swaziland, Tunisia, and Turkmenistan.

Roadblocks

The attempt to eliminate human trafficking must acknowledge roadblocks as they relate to human trafficking laws, their enforcement, and the conditions that facilitate the activity. Despite U.S. efforts to globalize anti-trafficking efforts, there is no consistency of definition across countries (Kelly & Regan, 2000). In addition, the laws that exist deal mainly with the trafficking of women, to whom the research in the area of trafficking has quite often been restricted (Chuang, 1998). In Ecuador, for example, a couple convicted of trafficking children for use in child pornography received a twenty-five-year prison sentence under one of the country's drug laws, which carried a more severe sentence than its child abuse laws (Morrissey, 2006).

The issue of consent often clouds legalities; individuals may enter a country willingly but then be forced into labor, prostitution, or pornography (Munro, 2006) and be deported if they are arrested (Ford, 2001). Also a roadblock to ending trafficking is that in many cases in underdeveloped countries, the profit to civil and public servants is immense, with few consequences for overlooking the trafficking of persons (Zhang & Chin, 2004). In addition, it has been suggested that if law enforcement targeted the trafficking network instead of the trafficking victims, there would be more of an impact in that through the elimination of one of the links in the criminal network, the organization would be disrupted and perhaps dissolved (Zhang & Chin, 2004). Finally, the fact that trafficking may occur within national borders is not always apparent in discussions on human trafficking and transportation over country borders (Barrett, 2000).

In terms of enforcing human trafficking laws, the efforts of police and social services vary by jurisdictional lines and along interests. Insofar as much of human trafficking is hidden behind a mask of fraudulent labor contracts (Bales, 2004), law enforcement often fails to confirm immigration papers and often operates under the philosophy that foreigners look the same or do not have rights (McGill, 2003; Obokata, 2003); hence, individuals may traffic others under the guise of family membership without interference or questions from law enforcement officials.

> Research suggests that the trafficking of humans is easier than the trafficking of drugs (Bales, 2004).

Another roadblock is that it is often not taken into account that trafficking may be the source of the individuals involved in prostitution, pornography, or child pornography (McCabe, 2007a). In addition, it has been suggested that the focus of social services is essentially those children under the age of sixteen and that victims in the sixteen to eighteen age range are not a concern (Somerset, 2001).

When conditions exist that facilitate criminal activity, it is difficult to reduce or end the activity. In many cases of human trafficking, the victims have consented to work in various occupations, such as prostitution, but soon become aware of the extent of their indebtedness, intimidation, or exploitation (Kelly & Regan, 2000). It is also not unusual for spouses to be involved in human trafficking (McCabe, 2007b); thus, another dynamics of threats and intimidation within the family structure may exist. Finally, it must be acknowledged that the trafficking of humans is easier than the trafficking of drugs (Bales, 2004) and that often for the victims of human trafficking, life was worse in their home countries, where they faced abuse, poverty, and wars (Williams & Vlassis, 2001; Taylor & Jamieson, 1999); therefore, they are more likely to subject themselves to this lifestyle of victimization in the hope that some day it will end and they will have a wonderful life in the United States.

Summary

I was born in the United States and sold into slavery by my mother when I was four. I spent the next twelve years as a slave of a sex trafficking ring for American businessmen. I visited the states of California, Oregon, New Jersey, Arizona, and New Mexico—all as a victim of sex trafficking (Salvation Army, 2003).

Trafficking in people is now considered the third most profitable activity for organized crime (Bell, 2001). In the United States, there are more and more cases of individuals being held against their will either for labor or for sex. With few opportunities in many of the source countries, and the perception of the United States as a "land of milk and honey," the trafficking of humans is expected to continue unless efforts are made to end this criminal activity.

Among the first problems that must be acknowledged when addressing human trafficking is the definition itself. Other problems include that there has been no method for collecting information on cases and that the involvement of children as victims of human trafficking is often not recognized.

During the twentieth century, there was no single department or agency in the United States responsible for collecting data on human trafficking or those offenses related to trafficking. In 1998, the U.S. government estimated that between 45,000 and 50,000 people were trafficked into the United States annually. By 2003, the number of individuals trafficked into the United States had been reduced to between 18,000 and 20,000.

On the international front, there have been, and continue to be, multiple efforts to reduce or eliminate human trafficking. NGOs such as the Global Survival Network and Human Rights Watch are leaders in the attempt to raise awareness and reduce incidents of human trafficking outside of U.S. borders. However, there is still a large disparity between the number of known cases and the estimate of trafficking in persons, with extrapolations of two to twenty times the number of known cases (Kelly & Regan, 2000).

The Universal Declaration of Human Rights (1948) states that all human beings are born free, that no one shall be held in slavery or servitude, and that everyone has the right to freedom of movement and to free choice of employ-ment. Human trafficking violates these most basic of rights.

The trafficking of humans for sex and labor is a problem that touches every country in one respect or another. Victims of human trafficking are men, women, and children. These victims are forced through either physical violence or threats of violence to provide goods and services for the profit of their traffickers. The U.S. government and many governments outside of the United States have identified human trafficking, a crime against humanity, as an activity to be eliminated.

Questions on Chapter 6

1. How is the definition of human trafficking problematic?
2. How has the United States become a leader in addressing the problem of human trafficking?
3. How has the topic of human trafficking been tied to today's theme of terrorism?
4. Once a victim of human trafficking has been identified, what sort of services or resources do they require?
5. What are some of the best practices to end human trafficking outside of the United States?

Questions for Further Thought

1. Is the United States making a difference in the fight to end human trafficking?
2. Would other countries be as interested in human trafficking if the United States had not provided the lead (or the penalties)?
3. How have other countries responded to U.S. pressure to end human trafficking?
4. How are the conditions in other countries different from U.S. condi-tions and, in some ways, more of a disadvantage in supporting their efforts to end human trafficking?
5. What would be the best plan to end human trafficking?

APPENDIX A:
AN EMPIRICAL ASSESSMENT
OF TIER COUNTRIES—A SEARCH
FOR ASSOCIATED DEMOGRAPHIC
CHARACTERISTICS

According to the U.S. Department of State's 2005 *Trafficking in Persons Report* (*TIP*), more than 700,000 people are trafficked across international borders every year for either forced labor or sexual exploitation. This is not a new type of criminal activity.

The United Nations has defined trafficking as "the recruitment, transfer, harboring, or receipt of persons by threat or use of force." Unfortunately, many nations have misunderstood or ignored the definition and failed to recognize or respond to the cases of human trafficking occurring within their own borders. As a result, in October 2000, the U.S. Congress passed, and President Bill Clinton signed, the Trafficking Victims Protection Act (TVPA) to provide a comprehensive definition of trafficking and to address these issues on the national and international levels (U.S. Department of State, 2004).

The TVPA not only identified the action of human trafficking but laid the framework for the creation of the Office to Monitor and Combat Trafficking in Persons under the U.S. Department of State located in Washington, DC. The responsibilities of this office include the classification of countries on the basis of their number of human trafficking cases and their responses to human trafficking. This classification system is the basis for the annual *TIP*.

The U.S. Office to Monitor and Combat Trafficking in Persons identified various tiers into which countries may be classified relative to their
efforts to comply with the TVPA and 2003 Trafficking Victims Protection
and Reauthorization Act (TVPRA). Tier 1 countries are defined as those
whose governments fully comply with the Act's minimum standards. Tier 2
countries are defined as those that do not fully comply with the Act's minimum
standards but are making significant efforts to bring themselves into compliance with those standards. Tier 3 countries are those that do not fully comply
with the minimum standards and are not making significant efforts to do so.
The TVPRA also created a special Watch List of countries to receive focused
attention during the following year. This special watch list was established for
countries in the Tier 2 classification that showed a significant number of victims
in the severe form of trafficking category, a significant increase in the number
of victims, or evidence that the country was failing to increase its efforts to
end human trafficking (Krause, 2006). For the classification of countries into
the various tiers, information is collected from U.S. embassies, consultants
around the world, foreign ambassadors in Washington, and nongovernmental
and international organizations working on human rights issues.

In the *2004 TIP*

1. twenty-five countries occupied Tier 1, including Australia, Austria,
    and the United Kingdom.
2. fifty-four countries occupied Tier 2, including Afghanistan, Bulgaria,
    Costa Rica, and Switzerland.
3. forty-two countries occupied the Tier 2 Watch List, including Bolivia,
    Greece, Honduras, and Zimbabwe.
4. ten countries occupied Tier 3, including Bangladesh, Cuba, North
    Korea, and Sudan.

For a complete list of the countries used in this analysis, see Table A.1.

The TVPA of 2000 laid the framework for all U.S. efforts against human
trafficking (Goodey, 2004). Today the three minimum standards for the TVPA
are that (1) the governments of countries should prohibit severe forms of trafficking in persons and should punish such acts and the persons responsible;
(2) the governments of countries should prescribe punishment for sex trafficking involving force similar to that of forcible sexual assault; and (3) the
governments of countries should punish any act that constitutes a severe form
of trafficking. For clarity, severe forms of trafficking include the sex trafficking

Table A.1. Countries by Tier Classification

Tier 1

Australia, Austria, Belgium, Canada, Colombia, Czech Republic, Denmark, France, Germany, Ghana, Hong Kong, Italy, Republic of Korea, Lithuania, Macedonia, Morocco, The Netherlands, New Zealand, Norway, Poland, Portugal, Spain, Sweden, Taiwan, and the United Kingdom

Tier 2

Afghanistan, Albania, Angola, Argentina, Armenia, Bahrain, Belarus, Benin, Bosnia, Brazil, Bulgaria, Burkina Faso, Burundi, Cambodia, Cameroon, Chile, China, Costa Rica, Egypt, El Salvador, Finland, The Gambia, Guinea, Hungary, Indonesia, Iran, Israel, Kuwait, Kyrgyz Republic, Latvia, Lebanon, Malaysia, Mali, Mauritius, Moldova, Mozambique, Nepal, Nicaragua, Niger, Panama, Romania, Rwanda, Saudi Arabia, Singapore, Slovak Republic, Slovenia, South Africa, Sri Lanka, Switzerland, Togo, United Arab Emirates, Uganda, Ukraine, and Uzbekistan

Tier 2 Watch

Azerbaijan, Belize, Bolivia, Democratic Republic of Congo, Côte d'Ivoire, Croatia, Cyprus, Dominican Republic, Estonia, Ethiopia, Gabon, Georgia, Greece, Guatemala, Honduras, India, Jamaica, Japan, Kazakhstan, Kenya, Laos, Madagascar, Malawi, Mauritania, Mexico, Nigeria, Pakistan, Paraguay, Peru, Philippines, Qatar, Russia, Senegal, Serbia-Montenegro, Suriname, Tajikistan, Tanzania, Thailand, Turkey, Vietnam, Zambia, and Zimbabwe

Tier 3

Bangladesh, Burma, Cuba, Ecuador, Equatorial Guinea, Guyana, North Korea, Sierra Leone, Sudan, and Venezuela

---

of children (those under the age of eighteen) and the use of fraud or coercion for the purpose of involuntary servitude, debt bondage, or slavery. The fourth standard, later amended in the 2003 TVPRA signed by President George W. Bush, states that governments should make serious and sustained efforts to eliminate human trafficking of all categories and calls for the use of ten criteria to assess whether a country is making such efforts.

Unfortunately, research on the subject of human trafficking is limited. Of the research that exists, the majority examines specific cases of human trafficking and does not provide intercountry analyses. Farr (2004) suggests that individuals living in poverty are more likely to be victims of human trafficking; however, Farr failed to provide empirical assessments of poverty relating to incidents of human trafficking. Raymond and Hughes (2001) suggest that women living in male-dominated societies are more likely to be victims of trafficking; however, these findings were based on a relatively small number of women involved in the sex trade. Poulin (2003) suggests that individuals living in densely populated countries with few financial opportunities tend to be victims of trafficking. Again, in neither case does the research provide a quantitative assessment of the links between financial opportunity and human trafficking. This appendix is an attempt to fill that gap. Specifically, the purpose is to compare demographic characteristics of countries ranked within the tier system to determine whether structural differences exist within the country rankings. I suggest that if specific structural elements could be identified as related to human trafficking, then proactive measures could be taken to improve those elements and therefore help to reduce or end human trafficking.

Methodology

The research approach in this study involved the use of secondary data in a cross-sectional design. Information was collected from the World Population Bureau for the year 2008, which was cross-referenced with the 2004 *TIP* report. The sample for this study consisted of 132 countries. (In the Tier 2 Watch List, Serbia and Montenegro were listed as one region. For this analysis, these countries' information was collected and analyzed separately.)

Country demographics were utilized in this study and examined in terms of three aspects: (1) poverty, (2) density, and (3) maleness. Variables operationalized to represent poverty were (1) immigrants per 1,000 population, (2) percentage unemployment, (3) life expectancy in years, and (4) infant mortality per 1,000 live births. Variables utilized to determine population density were population size and size of country in square miles. Density was calculated as population per square mile. Finally, the male to female population ratio was used to determine the maleness of a country.

Results

As shown in Table A.1, there were twenty-five countries in Tier 1, fifty-four countries in Tier 2, forty-three countries in the Tier 2 Watch List, and ten countries in Tier 3 used in this projects analysis. In an attempt to identify statistically significant differences in variables among tier classifications, analysis of variance (ANOVA) was used. As shown in Table A.2, there were significant differences ($p < 0.05$) for immigration, life expectancy, and infant mortality. Each of these variables was utilized to operationalize poverty.

Table A.2. ANOVA Results for Country Characteristic Variables of Tier 1, Tier 2, Tier 2 Watch List, and Tier 3 Categories

Variable	Mean (S.D.)	p-Value
Unemployment (%)		0.185
Tier 1	9.358 (7.2)	
Tier 2	11.359 (10.3)	
Tier 2 Watch List	14.022 (11.8)	
Tier 3	18.350 (21.5)	
Infant Mortality (per 1,000 live births)		0.000*
Tier 1	9.17 (11.7)	
Tier 2	27.82 (33.99)	
Tier 2 Watch List	34.89 (26.3)	
Tier 3	34.29 (22.6)	
Life Expectancy (years)		0.000*
Tier 1	77.7 (4.6)	
Tier 2	70.4 (10.6)	
Tier 2 Watch List	68.1 (8.3)	
Tier 3	69.0 (8.1)	
Immigrants (per 1,000 population)		0.016*
Tier 1	1.57 (1.85)	
Tier 2	0.77 (4.2)	
Tier 2 Watch List	–0.95 (4.1)	
Tier 3	–2.03 (2.9)	
Density (population per square mile)		0.449
Tier 1	1,085.2 (3,298.6)	
Tier 2	862.4 (2,858.5)	
Tier 2 Watch	247.9 (256.1)	
Tier 3	103.3 (98.9)	
Male to Female Population Ratio		0.610
Tier 1	0.9713 (0.03)	
Tier 2	1.008 (0.14)	
Tier 2 Watch	1.0261 (0.19)	
Tier 3	1.002 (0.02)	

* Statistically significant ($p < 0.05$).

Discussion

In comparing demographic characteristics among countries on the basis of their tier classifications, it was determined that certain variables are related to country classification. Specifically, the variables immigrants per 1,000 population, life expectancy in years, and infant mortality are all associated with tier classification. In general, the more migrants leave a country, the more likely the country will be classified as Tier 3 (with a problem of human trafficking and few efforts to reduce the problem). In addition, the lower the life expectancy of a country's residents, the more likely the country will be classified as Tier 3. Finally, the higher the infant mortality in a country, the more likely it is to be classified within Tier 3.

The United States is one of the most aggressive countries in its fight against human trafficking. As a result of U.S. legislation, there now exists the Office to Combat and Monitor Trafficking in Persons, charged with classifying countries based on their problems with and efforts to prevent human trafficking. In addition, the U.S. government provides grants to states, units of local government, Native American tribes, and nonprofit nongovernmental organizations to develop and strengthen services for trafficking victims across the globe.

APPENDIX B:
MEXICAN IMMIGRANTS

Historically, Ellis Island in New York was the main port of entry for immigrants into the United States; however, today the largest group of immigrants (both legal and illegal) into the United States is Mexican, and the entry points are not in New York but the southern borders of several states along the border between Mexico and the United States. It is these immigrants from Mexico that Census information documents increased from 2.6 million in 1990 to 4.9 million in 2000. These Mexican immigrants comprise 25% of all foreign-born workers in the United States (Greico & Ray, 2004). These Mexican immigrants are also quickly becoming one of the largest groups of human trafficking victims in the United States and they are the focus of this appendix.

The migration of Mexican immigrants into the United States began increasing in the early 1900s in response to the Mexican Revolution (Krissman, 2000). At that time, citizens of Mexico were pushed from their country, away from the poverty and destruction of their homeland, and pulled into the prosperity of the United States. During the U.S. Depression, Mexican migration into the United States slowed; however, the U.S. labor shortages of the 1940s World War II era saw the return of the Mexican immigrant into the country.

In the 1960s, the Bracero Program was an attempt to limit the number of immigrants (especially Mexicans) into the United States; however, labor demand remained great and those immigrants who could not enter the country legally began entering the United States illegally. In 1986, in response to the large number of illegal immigrants, the Immigration Reform and Control Act was passed and, for the first time, special efforts were made to seek out and punish those individuals employing illegal aliens (Weeks, 2002). Later, in 1996, the Illegal Immigrant Reform and Immigrant Responsibility Act was enacted to focus government attention on border protection and specifically on the deterring, finding, and deporting of illegal immigrants; however, there was little evidence of its effectiveness (Loaeza Tovar & Martin, 1997). In fact, many researchers found that in areas with large numbers of illegal aliens, the demand on social services was greater and crime and victimization had increased (Salant et al., 2001). Of course, the victimization focused on in this narrative is the victimization of human trafficking.

A Mexican trafficker used a *coyote* (smuggler) to bring women and children across the border with no documentation. After an eleven-day trip on foot into the United States, the women and girls were forced into prostitution in Florida and South Carolina (Richard, 1999).

During the 1960s and 1970s, there were approximately 300,000 illegal Mexicans in the United States; of those, approximately 5,000 were women. From 2000 to 2002, the estimated number of illegal Mexicans in the United States was 850,000, and of those more than 300,000 were women (Hernandez, 2002). One of the main reasons for the growing number of illegal Mexican immigrants into the United States is the sex trade. Over the past few years, the U.S. demand for women in the sex trade has increased by more than 50%, and those involved in sex trafficking are aware of this demand (Hernandez, 2002). To meet the demand, traffickers will often take women from Mexico into the United States, as it is the easiest country for access and, if traffickers are caught, Mexico provides fewer penalties than any other country (Beeks & Amir, 2006).

The United Nations as well as the United States defines trafficking as involving "the recruitment, transportation, harboring, or receipt of persons, by means of threats, force, or other forms of coercion." This definition suggests that anyone involved in the trafficking process is subject to penalties for human trafficking and also that trafficking is not limited to sexual exploitation but also includes labor.

In December 2004, the Federal Bureau of Investigation (FBI) launched the National Hispanic Sex Trafficking Initiative to stop sex traffickers who are bringing an increasing number of female victims into the United States from Mexico. Through this initiative, the FBI is collecting and sharing information on pending and closed cases, targeting Hispanic sex trafficking operations. The goal of this initiative is to identify the major traffickers and trafficking organizations and then through aggressive organization-focused efforts apprehend and prosecute the members of these criminal networks.

In Mexico, poverty rates are high and many Mexicans seek a better life in the United States. Unfortunately, for some Mexicans, the chance for a better life is quite expensive. *Coyotes*, the term used to describe the individuals who smuggle the Mexicans into the United States, may charge hundreds or even thousands of dollars. Individuals who do not have the money to pay the *coyote* at the time of transportation may be offered the opportunity to pay the *coyote* or a trafficker working with the *coyote* once they arrive in the United States. It is at this point, when individuals become indebted to another person and are forced or coerced into work they may not have chosen (such as prostitution, pornography, or stripping), that they have become victims of trafficking, and in particular the victims of sex trafficking.

Trafficking cases involving illegal Mexican immigrants, just as with cases involving other immigrants, are extremely difficult to detect. The crimes occur in environments of fear, there exist language barriers, and victims are often isolated (Acharya, 2005). The main destination for women and children from Mexico is the United States, to which approximately 5,000 young women are trafficked annually for the sex industry, agricultural labor, or domestic servitude (Acharya, 2005). Although the United States has acknowledged the problem of Mexican trafficking into the country, the criminal activity continues and practices such as voluntary prostitution and the 1994 conflict between the indigenous people of Mexico and the Mexican government fuel the problem (Beeks & Amir, 2006). Specifically, during the 1994 conflict, more than 40,000 individuals were forced to leave their homes and had few options for a quality life; hence, many chose to attempt to leave the country.

One way to traffic a young girl into the United States is through the promise of a good job. In many cases, her family will agree to this arrangement. Once she arrives in the United States, the traffickers take her passport and do not allow her to choose her line of work. Another way is by the use of a *coyote*, who may smuggle her across the border to later hold her against her will in exchange for a higher transportation fee. Of course, young women may also be bought by traffickers within Mexico for $400 to $800 and then resold in the United States for $5,000 to $10,000 (Beeks & Amir, 2006). Finally, one of the easiest ways to move a young woman from Mexico into the United States is to allow her to overstay her visa or "reuse" her visa. In Mexico, visas are valid for ten years; thus, many young women of similar physical characteristics will utilize a single visa. In addition, once a young girl is within the United States, she is difficult to detect; thus instead of returning to her country, she simply remains in the States even after the visa expires.

Since 1993, U.S. authorities have discovered several large underground tunnels used by both drug traffickers and human traffickers to move drugs and people from Mexico into the United States. In 2005, it was estimated that more than 3 million illegal immigrants had entered the United States in the previous five years (Wu, 2006). California was home to more illegal immigrants than any other state, with an estimate of 2.8 million illegal Mexican immigrants, followed by Texas with 1.4 million illegal Mexican immigrants. In addition, between 2000 and 2005, in Arizona the percentage of illegal Mexicans grew from 55% to 67%. Overall, in 2000, it was estimated that roughly one-half of the Mexican-born population in the United States was illegal (Camarota & McArdle, 2003). Of course, as these Mexican immigrants are illegal, they are at risk for victimization by traffickers in terms of labor and sexual exploitation without the perceived ability to seek assistance from the law enforcement community to end their abuse.

The main occupations for male illegal Mexican immigrants are as farm laborers and in construction. The main occupations for female illegal Mexican immigrants involve work in a private household as maids or as servants; however, there are many cases of forced prostitution. These illegal men and women also occupy positions in hotels, laundries, and sweatshops, often without the opportunity for change and without the opportunity to leave if they desire.

Mexico is a source, transit, and destination country for persons trafficked for both labor and sex. The majority of the victims trafficked into Mexico are from Central America, and the majority of the individuals trafficked from Mexico are en route to the United States. In addition, a significant number of Mexican children are trafficked internally for sexual exploitation. Sex tourism, especially tourism involving the abuse of minors, is a growing industry in Mexico as Americans and others from outside the country travel to Mexico to engage in sex with a child.

The Mexican government suggests that organized crime networks are involved in many aspects of human trafficking. They also report that often human trafficking is ignored by their authorities and that law enforcement as well as immigration officials are paid bribes by traffickers not to question or investigate the trafficking of victims. The country admits to the corruption of its officials, so it is no wonder human trafficking continues.

To illustrate the abhorrent conditions faced by some of these Mexican immigrants, take the case of *United States v. Paoletti* (1997). For nearly a decade, it is believed by U.S. authorities, the Paoletti family trafficked more than 1,000 deaf and mute Mexican immigrants to the United States. These immigrants were assured good jobs if they came to the United States; instead, they were forced to sell trinkets and beg in the subway stations of New York. They were held in conditions of slavery, constantly monitored, and punished (sometimes with stun guns) if they did not make their daily quotas or tried to escape. In 1997, members of the Paoletti crime family were convicted of aiding and abetting, conspiracy, the bringing in, transportation, harboring, and inducement to enter of illegal aliens, the interference in commerce by threats or violence, and involuntary servitude (Richard, 1999). It is estimated that the Paoletti family made more than $8 million before their arrest. The ringleader received the harshest sentence: fourteen years in prison. Although this case is nearly ten years old, the conditions facilitating this type of criminal activity have remained in place.

In all human trafficking cases, there is a victim and a trafficker. The victim is abused and lacks the ability to report the abuse. Although several nongovernmental organizations such as the Coalition Against Trafficking in Women and the Bilateral Border Safety Coalition are helping to reduce human trafficking in Mexico, traffickers have a vested interest (dollars) in maintaining the activity. As the United States experiences more and more Mexican immigrants entering the country (both legally and illegally), we should expect more and more Mexican immigrants to be identified as victims of human trafficking.

APPENDIX C:
A COMPARISON OF TIER 1
AND TIER 3 COUNTRIES

As stated in Appendix A, the U.S. Office to Monitor and Combat Trafficking has identified various tiers into which countries may be classified relative to their efforts to comply with the Trafficking Victims Protection Act (TVPA) of 2000. This appendix is a comparison of those countries identified as Tier 1 and Tier 3 to determine whether structural differences exist among the countries. If so, these structural differences may be related to the prevalence of human trafficking cases.

Methodology

The research approach in this study involved the use of secondary data in a cross-sectional design. Information was collected from the World Population Bureau for the year 2006, which was cross-referenced with the Office to Monitor and Combat Trafficking's 2004 *Trafficking in Persons* report. The sample for this study consisted of thirty-five countries. In all, seven country variables were utilized in this comparison. Those variables were (1) country region (Africa, East Asia, Eurasia, Near East, South Asia, Western hemisphere); (2) percentage unemployment; (3) infant mortality per 1,000 live births; (4) life expectancy in years; (5) immigrants per 1,000 population; (6) population density; and (7) male to female population ratio. For clarity, population density was calculated as population per square mile.

Results

As displayed in Table C.1, there were twenty-five countries in Tier 1 and ten countries in Tier 3. As displayed in Table C.2, the majority of the Tier 1 countries were located in Eurasia (64%). In comparison, the Tier 3 countries were located predominantly within Africa, East Asia, or the Western hemisphere.

In Tier 1 countries, life expectancy and migration into the country were higher, and the countries were more densely populated. In Tier 3 countries, unemployment and infant mortality were higher. The male to female population ratio was essentially the same; however, Tier 3 countries were slightly more likely to have a higher male to female ratio than Tier 1 countries.

Discussion

Certain variables are higher in Tier 1 countries and other variables are higher in Tier 3 countries. In general, those characteristics more related to the Tier 3 countries were related to poverty. Much of the literature discusses the association between poverty and human trafficking. This simple examination supports that association. Perhaps by proactively approaching the underlining condition of human trafficking, one can end the criminal activity.

Table C.1. Countries by Tier Classification

Tier 1
Australia, Austria, Belgium, Canada, Colombia, Czech Republic, Denmark, France, Germany, Ghana, Hong Kong, Italy, Republic of Korea, Lithuania, Macedonia, Morocco, The Netherlands, New Zealand, Norway, Poland, Portugal, Spain, Sweden, Taiwan, and the United Kingdom
Tier 3
Bangladesh, Burma, Cuba, Ecuador, Equatorial Guinea, Guyana, North Korea, Sierra Leone, Sudan, and Venezuela

Table C.2. Demographic Characteristics of Tier 1 and Tier 3 Countries

	Tier 1 (*n* = 25)	Tier 3 (*n* = 10)
Region (number)		
Africa	1 (4%)	3 (30%)
East Asia	5 (20%)	2 (20%)
Eurasia	16 (64%)	0 (0%)
Near East	1 (4%)	0 (0%)
South Asia	0 (0%)	1 (10%)
Western hemisphere	2 (8%)	4 (40%)
Unemployment (%)		
	Mean = 9.4	Mean = 18.4
	Median = 7.7	Median = 9.9
	Range = (3.7, 37.3)	Range = (1.9, 60.9)
Infant Mortality (per 1,000 live births)		
	Mean = 9.2	Mean = 34.3
	Median = 5.0	Median = 27.5
	Range = (3.0, 50.3)	Range = (6.2, 61.9)
Life Expectancy (years)		
	Mean = 77.2	Mean = 69.0
	Median = 78.8	Median = 70.2
	Range = (58.9, 81.6)	Range = (58.9, 77.4)
Immigrants (per 1,000 population)		
	Mean = 1.6	Mean = –2.0
	Median = 1.5	Median = –0.8
	Range = (–.87, 5.9)	Range = (–7.5, 0)
Density (population per square mile)		
	Mean = 1,085.2	Mean = 103.3
	Median = 292.8	Median = 99.4
	Range = (6.8, 16,446.5)	Range = (9.2, 265.9)
Male to Female Population Ratio		
	Mean = 0.97	Mean = 1.0
	Median = 0.97	Median = 1.01
	Range = (0.89, 1.04)	Range = (0.97, 1.02)

APPENDIX D:
A COMPARISON OF TIER 2
AND TIER 2 WATCH LIST
COUNTRIES—A NEED FOR BOTH?

Appendix A documents the criteria used by the U.S. Office to Monitor and Combat Trafficking in Persons in its annual *Trafficking in Persons* (TIP) report to classify countries. This appendix serves as a comparative analysis between Tier 2 and Tier 2 Watch List countries to identify any differences in the structural characteristics of the countries.

Methodology

The research approach in this study involved the use of secondary data in a cross-sectional design. Information was collected from the World Population Bureau for the year 2006, which was cross-referenced with the 2004 *TIP* report. The sample for this study consisted of ninety-seven countries in the Tier 2 and Tier 2 Watch List categories. (In the *TIP* report, Serbia and Montenegro were listed as one country. For this analysis, the countries' information was collected and analyzed separately.)

In all, seven country variables were utilized in this study: (1) region (Africa, East Asia, Eurasia, Near East, South Asia, Western hemisphere); (2) population density; (3) male to female population ratio; (4) immigrants per 1,000 population; (5) percentage unemployment; (6) life expectancy in years; and

(7) infant mortality per 1,000 live births. Variables used to determine density were population size and size of the country in square miles. Density was calculated as population per square mile.

Results

As shown in Table D.1, there were fifty-four countries in the Tier 2 category and forty-three countries in the Tier 2 Watch List category used in this analysis. To identify statistically significant differences in variables among tier classifications, chi-square tests of independence and Z-tests were used. As shown in Table D.2, there were no significant differences ($p < 0.05$) in terms of the information collected.

Discussion

No correlation was found to exist between the structural characteristics of a country and its ranking as either Tier 2 or Tier 2 Watch List. These results perhaps support the application of the ten criteria used to determine the rankings for countries within the tier system. Specifically, in distinguishing between Tier 2 and Tier 2 Watch List countries, perhaps the absolute number of victims of severe

Table D.1. Countries by Classification

Tier 2

Afghanistan, Albania, Angola, Argentina, Armenia, Bahrain, Belarus, Benin, Bosnia, Brazil, Bulgaria, Burkina Faso, Burundi, Cambodia, Cameroon, Chile, China, Costa Rica, Egypt, El Salvador, Finland, The Gambia, Guinea, Hungary, Indonesia, Iran, Israel, Kuwait, Kyrgyz Republic, Latvia, Lebanon, Malaysia, Mali, Mauritius, Moldova, Mozambique, Nepal, Nicaragua, Niger, Panama, Romania, Rwanda, Saudi Arabia, Singapore, Slovak Republic, Slovenia, South Africa, Sri Lanka, Switzerland, Togo, United Arab Emirates, Uganda, Ukraine, and Uzbekistan

Tier 2 Watch List

Azerbaijan, Belize, Bolivia, Democratic Republic of Congo, Côte d'Ivoire, Croatia, Cyprus, Dominican Republic, Estonia, Ethiopia, Gabon, Georgia, Greece, Guatemala, Honduras, India, Jamaica, Japan, Kazakhstan, Kenya, Laos, Madagascar, Malawi, Mauritania, Mexico, Nigeria, Pakistan, Paraguay, Peru, Philippines, Qatar, Russia, Senegal, Serbia-Montenegro, Suriname, Tajikistan, Tanzania, Thailand, Turkey, Vietnam, Zambia, and Zimbabwe forms of trafficking is statistically significant, perhaps assessments are applied on the progress countries are making to reduce human trafficking, and perhaps the actions by a country to bring itself into compliance with minimum standards is being considered by the Office to Monitor and Combat Trafficking in Persons. This study suggests that criteria other than country demographics are used in the placement of countries into the tier system, which is how it should be.

Table D.2. Demographic Characteristics of Tier 2 and Tier 2 Watch List Countries

	Tier 2 (*n* = 54)	Tier 2 Watch List (*n* = 43)	*p*-Value
Region (number)			0.616
Africa	14 (25.9%)	13 (30.2%)	
East Asia	6 (11.1%)	5 (11.6%)	
Eurasia	16 (29.6%)	12 (27.9%)	
Near East	8 (14.8%)	2 (4.7%)	
South Asia	3 (5.6%)	2 (4.7%)	
Western hemisphere	7 (13.0%)	9 (20.9%)	
Unemployment (%)			0.268
	Mean = 11.4	Mean = 14.0	
	Median = 8.4	Median = 9.5	
	Range = (1.6, 45.5)	Range = (2.0, 48.0)	
Infant Mortality (per 1,000 live births)			0.640
	Mean = 27.8	Mean = 34.9	
	Median = 16.6	Median = 24.9	
	Range = (2.3, 160.2)	Range = (6.7, 106.5)	
Life Expectancy (years)			0.445
	Mean = 70.4	Mean = 68.1	
	Median = 72.6	Median = 70.2	
	Range = (40.0. 81.7)	Range = (48.8. 77.8)	
Immigrants (per 1,000 population)			0.113
	Mean = 0.8	Mean = −0.95	
	Median = 0.0	Median = −0.42	
	Range = (−5.7, 15.7)	Range = (−8.8, 14.1)	
Density (population per square mile)			0.222
	Mean = 862.4	Mean = 247.9	
	Median = 205.3	Median = 158.2	
	Range = (37.4, 16,761.8)	Range = (7.0, 862.9)	
Male to Female Population Ratio			0.979
	Mean = 1.01	Mean = 1.03	
	Median = 0.97	Median = 1.00	
	Range = (0.86, 1.52)	Range = (0.84, 1.87)	

REFERENCES

Chapter 1

Beasley, D. (1918). Slavery in California. *Journal of Negro History*, 3 (1), 33–44.

Beeks, K. & Amir, D. (2006). *Trafficking and the Global Sex Industry*. Lanham, MD: Lexington Books.

Bell, R. (2001). Sex Trafficking: A Financial Crime Perspective. *Journal of Financial Crime*, 9 (2), 165–177.

Berlin, I. (1998). *Many Thousands Gone: The First Two Centuries of Slavery in North America*. Cambridge, MA: Harvard University Press.

Braudel, F. (2001). *The Perspective of the World, Vol III of Civilization and Capitalism*. London: Orion.

Doyle, R. (2006). Modern Slavery. *Scientific America*, January, p. 30.

Gallay, A. (2002). *The Indian Slave Trade: The Rise of the English Empire in the American South 1670–1671*. New Haven: Yale University Press.

Genealogy.com. (1999). White Slavery in 1800s in GA. August 5, 1999. Accessed at http://genforum.genealogy.com/ga/messages/3062.html on November 8, 2006.

International Organization for Migration (IOM). (1999). *Perspectives on Trafficking of Migrants: International Organization for Migration Foundation Against Trafficking in Women*. New York: Global Alliance Against Trafficking in Women.

Interpol. (2004). *People Smuggling*. Lyon, France: Interpol.

Lush, T. (2004). Modern-Day Slavery Hides Behind Florida's Doors. *St. Petersburg Times*, March 29, 2006, p. A1.

May, M. (2006). Diary of a Sex Slave. *San Francisco Chronicle*, October 8, p. A1.

Mirkinson, J. (1997). The Global Trade in Women. *Earth Island Journal*, 13 (1), 30–31.

Munro, V. (2006). Stopping Traffic? A Comparative Study of Responses to the Trafficking of Women for Prostitution. *British Journal of Criminology*, 46 (2), 318–333.

Piersen, W. (1988). *Black Yankees: The Development of an Afro-American Subculture in 18th Century New England*. Amherst, MA: University of Massachusetts.

Raymond, J. & Hughes, D. (2001). *Sex Trafficking of Women in the United States: International and Domestic Trends*. Amherst, MA: Coalition Against Trafficking in Women.

Richard, A. (1999, November). *International Trafficking in Women to the United States: A Contemporary Manifestation of Slavery and Organized Crime*. DCI Exceptional Intelligence Analyst Program of Intelligence Monograph. Washington, DC: Center for the Study of Intelligence.

United Nations Office on Drugs and Crime (UNODC). (2006, April). *Trafficking in Persons: Global Patterns*. UN: Human Trafficking Unit.

U.S. Department of State. (1997, August). *The Russian Maid Scheme*. Washington, DC: Bureau on Consumer Affairs, Office of Fraud Prevention Programs.

U.S. Department of State. (2003a, February). *Pathbreaking Strategies in the Global Fight against Sex Trafficking*. Washington, DC: U.S. Department of Justice.

U.S. Department of State. (2003b, August). *Assessments of US Activities to Combat Trafficking*. Washington, DC: U.S. Department of Justice.

U.S. Department of State. (2004, June). *Trafficking in Persons*. Report. Washington, DC: Office to Monitor and Combat Trafficking in Persons.

U.S. Department of State. (2005, July). *The Facts about Human Trafficking for Forced Labor*. Fact Sheet. Washington, DC: Office to Monitor and Combat Trafficking in Persons.

Williams, E. (1994). *Capitalism and Slavery*. Chapel Hill: University of North Carolina Press.

Chapter 2

Bales, K. (2004). *New Slavery: A Reference Handbook* (2nd edition). Santa Barbara, CA: ABC-CLIO.

Barkan, S. (2001). *Criminology: A Sociological Understanding* (2nd edition). Upper Saddle River, NJ: Prentice Hall.

Bell, R. (2001). Sex Trafficking: A Financial Crime Perspective. *Journal of Financial Crime*, 9 (2), 165–172.

Bertone, A. (2000). International Political Economy and the Politics of Sex. *Gender Issues*, 18 (1), 4–22.

Brown, H. (1999). Sex Crimes and Tourism in Nepal. *International Journal of Contemporary Hospitality Management*, 11 (23), 107–110.

CBSNews.com. (2006). IRS May Target Pimps. June 28, 2006. Accessed at http://www.cbsnews.com/stories/2006/06/28/politics/printable1762152.shtm on January 9, 2007.

Chesler, P. (1994). A Woman's Right to Self Defense: The Case of Aileen Carol Wuornos. In *Patriarchy Notes of an Expert Witness*, pp. 11–13. Monroe, MN: Common Courage.

Chin, K. (1999). *Smuggled Chinese: Clandestine Immigration to the United States*. Philadelphia, PA: Temple University Press.

Cullen, S. (2002). The Miserable Lives of Mail Order Brides. *Women in Action*, 3, 6–9.

de Vries, P. (2005). White Slaves in a Colonial Nation: The Dutch Campaign Against the Traffic in Women in the Early Twentieth Century. *Social and Legal Studies*, 14 (1), 39–60.

Doerner, W. & Lab, S. (2005). *Victimology* (4th edition). Columbus, OH: Anderson.

Doezema, J. (2005). Now You See Her, Now You Don't: Sex Workers at the UN Trafficking Protocol Negotiation. *Social and Legal Studies*, 14 (1), 61–89.

Farr, K. (2004). *Sex Trafficking: The Global Market in Women and Children*. New York: W. H. Freedman.

Goodey, J. (2004). Sex Trafficking in Women from Central and Eastern European Countries: Promoting a Victim-Centred and Woman-Centred Approach to Criminal Justice Intervention. *Feminist Review*, 76 (1), 26–45.

Guinn, D. & Steglich, E. (2003). *In Modern Bondage: Sex Trafficking in America*. Herndon, VA: Transnational.

Hotaling, G. & Finkelhor, D. (1988). *The Sexual Exploitation of Missing Children*. Washington, DC: U.S. Department of Justice.

Hughes, D. (2001). The Natasha Trade: Transnational Sex Trafficking. *National Institute of Justice Journal*, 246 (January 2001), pp. 9–14.

Hughes, D., Carlson, E., & Carlson, O. (2002). *Foreign Government Complicity in Human Trafficking: A Review of the State Department's 2002 Trafficking in Persons Report*. Report presented to the House Committee on International Relations, June 19, 2002.

Kangaspunta, K. (2006, April). *Trafficking in Persons: Global Patterns*. Vienna, Austria: United Nations Office on Drugs and Crime.

Lee, E. (1966). A Theory of Migration. *Demography*, 1, 47–57.

May, M. (2006a). US among Top 3 Destinations for Sex Trafficking in an $8B Trade. *Arizona Daily Star*, October 8, p. A1.

May, M. (2006b). Diary of a Sex Slave. *San Francisco Chronicle*, October 8, p. A1.

McCabe, K. (2003). *Child Abuse and the Criminal Justice System*. New York: Peter Lang.

McCabe, K. (2007a). Spousal Prostitution. In N. Jackson's (Ed.), *Encyclopedia of Domestic Violence*, pp. 673–674, New York: Routledge.

McCabe, K. (2007b). The Role of Internet Service Providers in Cases of Child Pornography and Child Prostitution. *Social Science Computer Review*, 25 (2), 1–5.

McGinnis, E. (2004). The Horrifying Reality of Sex Trafficking. Washington, DC: Concerned Women for America. December 12. Accessed at http://www.cwfa.org on November 12, 2006.

Miller, J. (2006). Modern Day Slavery. *Sheriff*, 58 (2), 34–36.

Miller, J. & Stewart, A. (1998). Report from the Roundtable on the Meaning of Trafficking in Persons: A Human Rights Perspective. *Women's Rights Law Reporter*, 20 (1), 1–12.

Mirkinson, J. (1997). The Global Trade in Women. *Earth Island Journal*, 13 (1), 30–31.

Poulin, R. (2003). Globalization and the Sex Trade: Trafficking and the Commodification of Women and Children. *Canadian Woman Studies*, 22 (3/4), 38–43.

Raymond, J. (2004). The Impact of the Sex Industry in the EU. Testimony before the European Parliament, January 2004. European Union.

Raymond, J. & Hughes, D. (2001). *Sex Trafficking of Women in the United States: International and Domestic Trends*. Amherst, MA: Coalition Against Trafficking in Women.

Richard, A. (1999, November). *International Trafficking in Women to the United States: A Contemporary Manifestation of Slavery and Organized Crime*. DCI Exceptional Intelligence Analyst Program of Intelligence Monograph. Washington, DC: Center for the Study of Intelligence.

Schauer, E. & Wheaton, E. (2006). Sex Trafficking into the United States: A Literature Review. *Criminal Justice Review*, 31 (2), 146–153.

Somerset, C. (2004). *Cause for Concern?* London: ECPAT.

Sulaimanova, S. (2006). Trafficking in Women from the Former Soviet Union for the Purpose of Sexual Exploitation. In K. Beeks & D. Amir (Eds.), *Trafficking and the Global Sex Industry*, pp.61–76. Lanham, MD: Lexington Books.

Taylor, I. & Jamieson, R. (1999). Sex Trafficking and the Mainstream of Market Culture. *Crime, Law, and Social Change*, 32 (3), 257–278.

Tiefenbrun, S. W. (2002). Sex Sells but Drugs Don't Talk: Trafficking of Women Sex Workers and an Economic Solution. *Thomas Jefferson Law Review*, 24 (2), 161–189.

U.S. Department of State. (2004a, June). *Trafficking in Persons*. Report. Washington, DC: Office to Monitor and Combat Trafficking in Persons.

U.S. Department of State. (2004b, March). *Recent Developments in US Government Efforts to End Human Trafficking*. Washington, DC: Office to Monitor and Combat Trafficking in Persons.

U.S. Department of State. (2005, July). *The Facts about Human Trafficking for Forced Labor*. Fact Sheet. Washington, DC: Office to Monitor and Combat Trafficking in Persons.

Wiehl, L. (2006). Trafficking. June 9, 2006. Accessed at http://www.foxnews.com on November 28, 2006.

Zimmerman, C. (2003). *The Health Risks and Consequences of Trafficking in Women and Adolescents*. London: London School of Hygiene and Tropical Medicine.

Chapter 3

Bales, K. & Lize, S. (2007). Investigating Human Trafficking. Challenges, Lessons Learned, and Best Practices. *FBI Law Enforcement Bulletin*, 76 (4), 24–32.

Center for Immigration Studies (CIS). (2001). Labor Market Characteristics of Mexican Immigrants in the United States. Accessed at http://www.cis.org/articles/2001/mexico/labor.html on January 1, 2007.

CNN.com. (2003). Labor Trafficking Cases Bring Penalties. February 22, 2003. Accessed at http://www.cnn.com/203/US/02/22/cheaplabor.ap/index.html on January 8, 2007.

Crandall, M., Senturia, K., Sullivan, M., & Shiu-Thornton, S. (2005). No Way Out: Russian-Speaking Women's Experiences with Domestic Violence. *Journal of Interpersonal Behavior*, 20 (8), 941–958.

Egan, T. (1996). Mail-Order Marriage, Immigrant Dreams and Death. *New York Times*, May 26, p. 12.

Galson, D. (1981). *White Servitude in Colonial America: An Economic Analysis*. Cambridge: Cambridge University Press.

Human Rights Watch (HRW). (2006). *Treatment of Migrant Domestic Workers with Special Visas in the United States*. New York: HRW.

International Labour Office. (2005). *A Global Alliance Against Forced Labor, Global Report under the Follow-up to the ILO Declaration on Fundamental Principles and Rights at Work 2005* (92-2-115360-6). Geneva, IL: ILO.

Kangaspunta, K. (2006, April). *Trafficking in Persons: Global Patterns*. Vienna, Austria: United Nations Office on Drugs and Crime.

Kolchin, P. (1993). *American Slavery 1619–1877*. New York: Hill and Wang.

Lush, T. (2004). Modern-Day Slavery Hides Behind Florida's Doors. *St. Petersburg Times*, March 29, p. A1.

McCabe, K. (2007). The Role of Internet Service Providers in Cases of Child Pornography and Child Prostitution. *Social Science Computer Review*, 25 (2), 1–5.

McCabe, K. & Martin, G. (2005). *School Violence, the Media, and Criminal Justice Responses*. New York: Peter Lang.

Miller, J. (2006). Modern Day Slavery. *Sheriff*, 58 (2), 34–36.

Munro, V. (2006). Stopping Traffic? A Comparative Study of Responses to the Trafficking of Women for Prostitution. *British Journal of Criminology*, 46 (2), 318–333.

National Institute of Justice. (2004, August). *Research in Brief*. Washington, DC: U.S. Department of Justice.

Organized Crime Digest. (2006). Iowa: Governor Outlaws Human Trafficking. *Organized Crime Digest*, 27 (8), 7.

Pehar, J. (2003). E-Bride. The Mail-Order Bride Industry and the Internet. *Canadian Woman Studies*, 22 (3/4), 171–175.

Richard, A. (1999, November). *International Trafficking in Women to the United States: A Contemporary Manifestation of Slavery and Organized Crime*. DCI Exceptional Intelligence Analyst Program of Intelligence Monograph. Washington, DC: Center for the Study of Intelligence.

TurkishPress.com. (2006). US Club Owner Gets 10 Years for Forced Labor, Trafficking. Accessed at http://www.turkishpress.com/news.asp?id=147230 on January 10, 2007.

U.S. Department of Health and Human Services. (2005). *Labor Trafficking*. Fact Sheet. Washington, DC: Rescue and Restore Victims of Human Trafficking.

U.S. Department of State. (2004a, June). *Trafficking in Persons*. Report. Washington, DC: Office to Monitor and Combat Trafficking in Persons.

U.S. Department of State. (2004b, March). *Recent Developments in US Government Efforts to End Human Trafficking*. Washington, DC: Office to Monitor and Combat Trafficking in Persons.

U.S. Department of State. (2005, July). *The Facts about Human Trafficking for Forced Labor*. Fact Sheet. Washington, DC: Office to Monitor and Combat Trafficking in Persons.

Chapter 4

Bales, K. & Lize, S. (2007). Investigating Human Trafficking. Challenges, Lessons Learned, and Best Practices. *FBI Law Enforcement Bulletin*, 76 (4), 24–32.

Bodenheimer, D. (2003). Technology for Border Protection: Homeland Security Funding and Priorities. Accessed at http://www.homelandsecurity.org/journal/articles/displayarticle.asp?article=95 on July 9, 2005.

Free the Slaves & The Human Rights Center. (2006). *The Challenge of Hidden Slavery: Legal Responses to Forced Labor in the United States*. Berkeley: University of California Press.

Goodey, J. (2003). Migration, Crime and Victimhood: Responses to Sex Trafficking. *Punishment and Society*, 5 (4), 415–421.

Hindustantimes.com. (2006). India Placed on US Special Watch List Against Slavery. June 6, 2006. Accessed at http://www.hindustantimes.com/news/181_1714046,00050001.htm on January 15, 2007.

King, G. (2004). *Woman, Child for Sale: The New Slave Trade in the 21st Century*. New York: Chamberlain Bros.

Krause, S. (2006). Burma, North Korea, Laos Fail to Stop Human Trafficking, US Says China, Indonesia, Malaysia, Cambodia among Those on Special Watch List. Washington, DC: USInfostate.gov. Accessed at http://usinfo.state.gov on January 15, 2007.

Miller, J. (2006). Modern Day Slavery. *Sheriff*, 58 (2), 34–36.

National Criminal Intelligence Services (NCIS). (2005). United Kingdom Threat Assessment of Serious and Organised Crime 2003. Accessed at http://www.ncis.co.uk/ukta/2003/threat04.asp on April 30, 2005.

News and Advance. (2005). US Blames 14 Nations of Not Stopping Human Trafficking. June 4, Lynchburg, VA: News and Advance, p. A2.

Somerset, C. (2004). *Cause for Concern? London Social Services and Child Trafficking*. London: ECPAT.

Sundberg, K. (2004). *Transitions in Canada's Border Security*. Master's thesis, Royal Roads University, British Columbia.

Sundberg, K. & Winterdyk, J. (2006). Border Security: Good Fences Make Good Neighbors. *Crime and Justice International*, 22 (91), 19–21.

Tiefenbrun, S. W. (2002). Sex Sells but Drugs Don't Talk: Trafficking of Women Sex Workers and an Economic Solution. *Thomas Jefferson Law Review,* 24 (2), 161–189.

Times of India. (2005). Human Traffickers Preying on Kids in Aceh: UNICEF. *The Times of India,* January 4, 1.

U.S. Department of Labor. (2002). *Trafficking in Persons: A Guide for Non-Governmental Organizations.* Washington, DC: Women's Bureau of the U.S. Department of Labor.

U.S. Department of State. (2004, March). *Recent Developments in US Government Efforts to End Human Trafficking.* Washington, DC: Office to Monitor and Combat Trafficking in Persons.

Zhang, S. & Chin, K. (2004). *Characteristics of Chinese Human Smugglers. NIJ Research in Brief.* Washington, DC: National Institute of Justice (NCJ 204989).

Chapter 5

Andrews, S. (2004). US Domestic Prosecution of the American International Sex Tourist: Efforts to Protect Children from Sexual Exploitation. *Journal of Criminal Law and Criminology,* 94 (2), 415–453.

Armentrout, D. (2002). Child Trafficking Continues to Threaten Young Women in India. Digital Freedom Network. Accessed at http://www.asiaobserver.com/India-story3.htm on February 8, 2006.

Associated Press. (2007). Girls Urge Action against Slavery, Child Labor. *Greenville News,* March 4, p. 13A.

Bales, K. (2000). *Disposable People.* Irvine, CA: University of California.

Bales, K. (2004). *New Slavery: A Reference Handbook* (2nd edition). Santa Barbara, CA: ABC–CLIO.

Barnitz, L. (2000). *Commercial Sexual Exploitation of Children.* Washington, DC: Youth Advocate Program.

BBCNews.com. (2003). *Organ Traffic Link in Mexico Murders.* May 1, 2005. Accessed at http://newsvote.bbc.co.uk on August 6, 2006.

Binh, V. (2006). Trafficking of Women and Children in Vietnam: Current Issues and Problems. In K. Beeks & D. Amir (Eds.), *Trafficking and the Global Sex Industry,* pp. 33–46. Lanham, MD: Lexington Books.

Campagne, D. & Poffenberger, D. (1988). *The Sexual Trafficking in Children.* Westport, CT: Auburn House.

Chidley, J., Paras, W., & Chu, S. (1996). Fighting the Child Sex Trade: Focus in an Ancient Evil. *World Press Review,* 43 (11), 6–8.

Corrections Digest. (2006). Research on Sexual Exploitation of Minors. *Corrections Digest,* 37 (2), 9.

Davidson, J. (2005). *Children in the Global Sex Trade.* Cambridge: Polity Press.

ECPAT. (2007). Info ECPAT. *ECPAT Groups' Monthly Newsletter,* March 20, p. 4. Washington, DC: ECPAT.

ECPAT-USAnews. (2007, January). *Does the US Protect Children from Commercial Sexual Exploitation.* New York: ECPAT-USAnews.

Ejalu, W. (2006). From Home to Hell: The Telling Story of an African Woman's Journey and Stay in Europe. In K. Beeks & D. Amir (Eds.), *Trafficking and the Global Sex Industry,* pp. 165–186. Lanham, MD: Lexington.

Estes, R. & Weiner, N. (2001). *The Commercial Sexual Exploitation of Children in the US, Canada, and Mexico.* Philadelphia, PA: University of Pennsylvania.

Farr, K. (2004). *Sex Trafficking: The Global Market in Women and Children*. New York: W. H. Freedman.

Kangaspunta, K. (2006, April). *Trafficking in Persons: Global Patterns*. Vienna, Austria: United Nations Office on Drugs and Crime.

King, R. (2002). Towards a New Map of European Migration. *International Journal of Population Geography*, 8, 89–106.

Lazaroiu, S. & Alexandru, M. (2003). *Who Is the Next Victim?* Oslo, Norway: International Organization for Migration.

McCabe, K. (2003). *Child Abuse and the Criminal Justice System*. New York: Peter Lang.

McCabe, K. (2007). The Role of Internet Service Providers in Cases of Child Pornography and Child Prostitution. *Social Science Computer Review*, 25 (2), 1–5.

Melrose, M. (2002). Labour Pains: Some Considerations of the Difficulties of Researching Juvenile Prostitution. *International Journal of Social Research Methodology, Theory, and Practice*, 5 (4), 333–351.

Miko, F. (2004). *Trafficking in Women and Children: The US and International Response*. Washington, DC: Library of Congress.

Miles, N. (2003). Organ Traffic Link in Mexico Murders. BBC News. May 1, 2003. Accessed at http://newsvote.bbc.co.uk on August 6, 2006.

Miller, J. (2006). Modern Day Slavery. *Sheriff*, 58 (2), 34–36.

Mirkinson, J. (1997). The Global Trade in Women. *Earth Island Journal*, 13 (1), 30–31.

Morrissey, S. (2006). Sinister Industry. *ABA Journal*, 92, 59–61.

Munro, V. (2006). Stopping Traffic? A Comparative Study of Responses to the trafficking of Women for Prostitution. *British Journal of Criminology*, 46 (2), 318–333.

National Criminal Intelligence Services (NCIS). (2005). United Kingdom Threat Assessment of Serious and Organised Crime 2003. Accessed at http://www.ncis.co.uk/ukta/2003/threat 04.asp on April 30, 2005.

Organized Crime Digest. (2006). Iowa: Governor Outlaws Human Trafficking. *Organized Crime Digest*, 27 (8), 7.

Richard, A. (1999, November). *International Trafficking in Women to the United States: A Contemporary Manifestation of Slavery and Organized Crime*. DCI Exceptional Intelligence Analyst Program of Intelligence Monograph. Washington, DC: Center for the Study of Intelligence.

Schauer, E. & Wheaton, E. (2006). Sex Trafficking into the United States: A Literature Review. *Criminal Justice Review*, 31 (2), 146.

Skeldon, R. (2000). Perspectives on Trafficking Migrants. *International Migration*, 38 (3), 99–115.

Somerset, C. (2001). *What the Professionals Know: The Trafficking of Children into, and through, the UK for Sexual Purposes*. London: ECPAT.

Somerset, C. (2004). *Cause for Concern?* London: ECPAT.

Spangenberg, M. (2002). *International Trafficking of Children to New York City for Sexual Purposes*. New York: ECPAT-USA.

UNICEF. (2006). *Trafficking and Sexual Exploitation. Child Protection from Violence, Exploitation, and Abuse*. Accessed at http://www.unicef.org/protection/index_exploitation.html on December 31, 2006.

U.S. Department of State. (2004, March). *Recent Developments in US Government Efforts to End Human Trafficking*. Washington, DC: Office to Monitor and Combat Trafficking in Persons.

U.S. Department of State. (2005, August 19). *The Facts about Child Sex Tourism*. Fact Sheet. Washington, DC: Office to Monitor and Combat Trafficking in Persons.

Van Impe, K. (2000). People for Sale: The Need for a Multidisciplinary Approach to Human Trafficking. *International Migration*, 38 (3), 99–115.

Youth Advocate Program International. (2004). Worst Forms of Child Labor/Modern Child Slavery. Accessed at http://www.yapi.org/slavery/ on March 5, 2006.

Zoba, W. (2003). The Hidden Slavery. *Christianity Today*, November, pp. 68–74.

Chapter 6

Bales, K. (2004). *New Slavery: A Reference Handbook* (2nd edition). Santa Barbara, CA: ABC–CLIO.

Banerjee, U. (2006). Migration and Trafficking of Women and Children: A Brief Review of Some Effective Models in India and Thailand. In K. Beeks & D. Amir (Eds.), *Trafficking and the Global Sex Industry*. Lanham, MD: Lexington Books.

Barnitz, L. (2000). *Commercial Sexual Exploitation of Children*. Washington, DC: Youth Advocate Program.

Barrett, D. (2000). *Youth Prostitution in the New Europe: The Growth of Sex Work*. London: Russell House.

Beeks, K. & Amir, D. (2006). *Trafficking and the Global Sex Industry*. Lanham, MD: Lexington Books.

Bell, R. (2001). Sex Trafficking: A Financial Crime Perspective. *Journal of Financial Crime*, 9 (2), 165–177.

Campagne, D. & Poffenberger, D. (1988). *The Sexual Trafficking in Children*. Westport, CT: Auburn House.

Chaikin, R. (2006). Fighting against Trafficking in Women in the North of Israel. In K. Beeks & D. Amir (Eds.), *Trafficking and the Global Sex Industry*, pp. 201–216. Lanham, MD: Lexington.

Chuang, J. (1998). Redirecting the Debate over Trafficking Women: Definitions, Paradigms, and Contexts. *Harvard Human Rights Journal*, 11 (1), 65–107.

Crandall, M., Senturia, K., Sullivan, M., & Shiu-Thornton, S. (2005). No Way Out: Russian-Speaking Women's Experiences with Domestic Violence. *Journal of Interpersonal Behavior*, 20 (8), 941–958.

ECPAT. (2007). Info ECPAT. *ECPAT Groups' Monthly Newsletter*, March 20, p. 4. Washington, DC: ECPAT.

Farr, K. (2004). *Sex Trafficking: The Global Market in Women and Children*. New York: W. H. Freedman.

Ford, M. (2001). *Sex Slaves and Legal Loopholes: Exploring the Legal Framework and Federal Responses to the Trafficking of Thai Contract Girls for Sexual Exploitation to Melbourne, Australia*. A Research Study. Melbourne: Project Respect.

Gallagher, A. (2006). Human Rights and Human Trafficking in Thailand: A Shadow Tip Report. In K. Beeks & D. Amir (Eds.), *Trafficking and the Global Sex Industry*, pp. 139–164. Lanham, MD: Lexington Books.

Junger, S. (2002). Slaves of the Brothel. *Vanity Fair*, July, pp. 112–117.

Jurado, D. (2005). Wising Up on Sexual Trafficking of Women and Children. *Freeman*, October 24, 2005. Accessed at http://www.thefreeman.com on June 15, 2006.

Kelly, L. & Regan, L. (2000). *Stopping Traffic: Exploring the Extent of, and Responses to, Trafficking Women for Sexual Exploitation in the UK*. Police Research Series. London: Home Office.

McCabe, K. (2007a). The Role of Internet Service Providers in Cases of Child Pornography and Child Prostitution. *Social Science Computer Review*, 25 (2), 1–5.

McCabe, K. (2007b). Spousal Prostitution. In N. Jackson's (Ed.), *Encyclopedia of Domestic Violence*, pp. 673–674, New York: Routledge.

McGill, C. (2003). *Human Traffic: Sex, Slaves and Immigration*. London: Vision.

Melrose, M. (2002). Labour Pains: Some Considerations of the Difficulties of Researching Juvenile Prostitution. *International Journal of Social Research Methodology, Theory, and Practice*, 5 (4), 333–351.

Miko, F. (2004). *Trafficking in Women and Children: The US and International Response*. Washington, DC: Library of Congress.

Morrissey, S. (2006). Sinister Industry. *ABA Journal*, 92, 59.

Munro, V. (2006). Stopping Traffic? A Comparative Study of Responses to the Trafficking of Women for Prostitution. *British Journal of Criminology*, 46 (2), 318–333.

Obokata, T. (2003). Human Trafficking, Human Rights, and the Nationality, Immigration, and Asylum Act 2002. *European Human Rights Law Review*, 4 (2), 410–422.

O'Connell-Davidson, J. (2002). *The Borders of Contract: Trafficking and Migration*. ESBC Seminar Series. University of Warwick, February 2.

Pinder J. (2001). *The European Union: A Very Short Introduction*. Oxford: Oxford University Press.

Ruiz-Austria, C. (2006). Conflicts and Interests: Trafficking in Filipino Women. In K. Beeks & D. Amir (Eds.), *Trafficking and the Global Sex Industry*, pp. 97–118. Lanham, MD: Lexington Books.

Salvation Army. (2003). *Human Trafficking Modern Day Slavery in America*. Washington, DC: Salvation Army.

Somerset, C. (2001). *What the Professionals Know: The Trafficking of Children into, and through, the UK for Sexual Purposes*. London: ECPAT.

Somerset, C. (2004). *Cause for Concern?* London: ECPAT.

Taylor, I. & Jamieson, R. (1999). Sex Trafficking and the Mainstream of Market Culture. *Crime, Law, and Social Change*, 32 (3), 257–278.

U.S. Department of State. (2003a, February). *Pathbreaking Strategies in the Global Fight against Sex Trafficking*. Washington, DC: U.S. Department of Justice.

U.S. Department of State. (2003b, August). *Assessments of US Activities to Combat Trafficking*. Washington, DC: U.S. Department of Justice.

U.S. Department of State. (2003c, November). *The US Government's International Anti-Trafficking Programs*. Washington, DC: U.S. Department of Justice.

U.S. Department of State. (2004, March). *Recent Developments in US Government Efforts to End Human Trafficking*. Washington, DC: Office to Monitor and Combat Trafficking in Persons.

Williams, P. & Vlassis, D. (2001). *Combating International Crime*. London: Frank Cass.

Zhang, S. & Chin, K. (2004). *Characteristics of Chinese Human Smugglers NIJ Research in Brief*. Washington, DC: National Institute of Justice (NCJ 204989).

Appendix A

Farr, K. (2004). *Sex Trafficking: The Global Market in Women and Children*. New York: W. H. Freedman.

Goodey, J. (2004). Sex Trafficking in Women from Central and Eastern European Countries: Promoting a Victim-Centred and Woman-Centred Approach to Criminal Justice Intervention. *Feminist Review*, 76 (1), 26–45.

Krause, S. (2006). Burma, North Korea, Laos Fail to Stop Human Trafficking, US Says China, Indonesia, Malaysia, Cambodia among Those on Special Watch List. Washington, DC: USInfostate.gov. Accessed at http://usinfo.state.gov on January 15, 2007.

Poulin, R. (2003). Globalization and the Sex Trade: Trafficking and the Commodification of Women and Children. *Canadian Woman Studies, 22* (3/4), 38–43.

Raymond, J. & Hughes, D. (2001). *Sex Trafficking of Women in the United States. International and Domestic Trends.* Amherst, MA: Coalition Against Trafficking in Women.

U.S. Department of State. (2004). *Trafficking in Persons Report, June 2004.* Washington, DC: Office to Monitor and Combat Trafficking in Persons.

U.S. Department of State. (2005). *The Facts about Human Trafficking for Forced Labor.* Fact Sheet. Washington, DC: Office to Monitor and Combat Trafficking in Persons, U.S. Department of State.

Appendix B

Acharya, A. (2005). *Law Esclavitud Humana: El Trafico de Mujeres en la India y Mexico.* Ph.D. dissertation, Universidad Nacional Autónoma de Mexico.

Acharya, A. (2006). International Migration and Trafficking of Mexican Women to the United States. In K. Beeks & D. Amir (Eds.), *Trafficking and the Global Sex Industry,* pp. 21–32. Lanham, MD: Lexington Books.

Beeks, K. & Amir, D. (2006). *Trafficking and the Global Sex Industry.* Lanham, MD: Lexington Books.

Camarota, S. A. & McArdle, N. (2003, September). *Where Immigrants Live: An Examination of State Residency of the Foreign Born by Country of Origin in 1990 and 2000.* Washington, DC: Center for Immigration Studies.

Greico, E. & Ray, B. (2004, March). *Mexican Immigrants in the US Labor Force. Migration Information Source.* Washington, DC: Migration Policy Institutes.

Hernandez, R. (2002). *La Migración, el Tema Incomodó de la Binacional.* Mexico: Milenio Diario.

Krissman, F. (2000). Immigration Labor Recruitment: Agribusiness and Undocumented Migration from Mexico. In N. Foner, R. Rumbaut, & S. Golds (Eds.), *Immigration Research for a New Century: Multidisciplinary Perspectives.* New York: Sage.

Loaeza Tovar, E. & Martin, S. (1997). *Migration between Mexico and the United States: A Report of the Binational Study of Migration.* Washington, DC: U.S. Commission on Immigration Reform.

Richard, A. (1999, November). *International Trafficking in Women to the United States: A Contemporary Manifestation of Slavery and Organized Crime.* DCI Exceptional Intelligence Analyst Program of Intelligence Monograph. Washington, DC: Center for the Study of Intelligence.

Salant, T., Brenner, C., Rubaii-Barrett, N., & Weeks, J. (2001). *Illegal Immigrant in US-Mexico Border Counties: Costs for Law Enforcement, Criminal Justice, and Emergency Medical Services.* San Diego, CA: Border Counties Coalition.

Weeks, J. (2002). *Population: An Introduction to Concepts & Issues* (8th edition). Belmont, CA: Wadsworth.

Wu, A. (2006, November). Fact Sheet: Border Apprehensions, 2005. Washington, DC: Office of Immigration Statistics.

INDEX